FUGITIVE VISIONS

ALSO BY JANE JEONG TRENKA

The Language of Blood: A Memoir

Outsiders Within: Writing on Transracial Adoption, editor,
with Julia Chinyere Oparah and Sun Yung Shin

Fugitive Visions

AN ADOPTEE'S RETURN TO KOREA

Jane Jeong Trenka

—◀○▶—

Graywolf Press
SAINT PAUL, MINNESOTA

Publication of this volume is made possible in part by a grant provided by the Minnesota State Arts Board, through an appropriation by the Minnesota State Legislature; a grant from the Wells Fargo Foundation Minnesota; and a grant from the National Endowment for the Arts, which believes that a great nation deserves great art. Significant support has also been provided by the Bush Foundation; Target; the McKnight Foundation; and other generous contributions from foundations, corporations, and individuals. To these organizations and individuals we offer our heartfelt thanks.

Published by Graywolf Press
2402 University Avenue, Suite 203
Saint Paul, Minnesota 55114
All rights reserved.

www.graywolfpress.org

Published in the United States of America

ISBN 978-1-55597-529-6

2 4 6 8 9 7 5 3 1
First Graywolf Printing, 2009

Library of Congress Control Number: 2008941979

Cover design: Jeenee Lee Design

Cover photo: Jane Jeong Trenka

For Rev. Do Hyun Kim and Jung Ae Kong

—◀o▶—

In each fugitive vision I see worlds,
Full of the changing play of rainbows . . .

—Konstantin Dmitrieyevich Balmont

FUGITIVE VISIONS

Chapter One

—◂o▸—

The first time I came to America, I met my adoptive parents.

The first time I returned to Korea, I met my Korean mother and sisters.

The second time I returned to Korea, I met my brother.

The third time I returned to Korea, my Korean mother was dying.

The fourth time I returned to Korea, I was newly married.

The fifth time I returned to Korea, I thought I could burn Korea out of my system and then return to my American life.

The sixth time I came to Korea, I was newly divorced.

오다: *oda:* to come

가다: *kada:* to go

돌다: *dolda:* to turn around

돌아오다: *dolaoda:* to turn around/return/come

돌아가다: *dolakada:* to turn around/return/go

돌아가시다: *dolakashida:* Polite/honorific for "to die," e.g.,
"When did your mother die?"

ASSUME A POINT OF REFERENCE, THEN CHOOSE THE CORRECT WORD:

When do you return (돌아오다/돌아가다) to America?

When do you return (돌아오다/돌아가다) to Korea?

When do you return (돌아오다/돌아가다) home?

고향: *kohyang:* one's home; one's hometown; one's native place; one's
birthplace; one's home country (village).

제 2의 고향: *je ieui kohyang:* one's second home; one's land of adoption; one's adopted land.

고향 *gohyang* is the pronunciation of a Sino-Korean word made of
two Chinese characters: 故 (고) *go* (cause, reason) + 鄉 (향) *hyang*
(countryside).

My short-lived marriage and my American life nearly three years behind me, I live in Seoul like a student, or a monk, in a room measuring
five meters one way and five the other, a refrigerator and gas stove on
an unheated veranda, a bathroom with no shower stall but a hose with
a showerhead attached. My few possessions include three cups, one

rice cooker, a sleeping mat, the books I didn't sell or give away to piano students or friends, the absence of a piano.

Yeonhuidong is a foreigner neighborhood and Korean neighborhood, a rich neighborhood and a poor neighborhood. The Seoul Foreign School, with both British and American divisions, as well as the Chinese school, are a ten-minute walk up the main street. The take-out chicken restaurant owners, the man who irons shirts in the window of the dry cleaner, the seamstress, the students, the shoe repair man, a Pakistani couple, white Westerners, and I live across the street from two former South Korean presidents. On the presidential side of the street is the bakery that sells whole wheat bread and passable baguettes; there's a grocery store with a whole aisle full of European cheese and American canned products, celery, an occasional lime, and stacks piled high with goods imported by a woman who most likely has a Korean American sister—simply ask for what you need in English and you shall receive the rare goods, for a price: Listerine, multivitamins, NyQuil, Quaker Instant Oats, packets of yeast. Next to her heap of goods is another, but that woman's sister apparently lives in Japan. Welcome to Yeonhuidong, called a *booja* neighborhood—a rich man's neighborhood—by Koreans who don't live here, even though in my alley at the end of the street, houses that look like they're straight from the countryside are still standing, their clay roofs decaying, the bars on the windows rusting. I live in Yeonhuidong because here Korean people are less afraid of foreigners, because these foreigners are from the U.S. State Department, not the Department of Defense, because I found a room, rare in Seoul, with two sunny windows that open, and because Yeonhuidong is so close to Sinchon and Hongdae, where the adopted Koreans drink. In one of the bars, they speak English. In the other, they speak French.

Across the alley from my apartment is Liberteville, the building where the truly rich foreigners live, their perfectly clean BMWs and Saabs humming in and out of the garage all day. Every morning the Korean guard, in a uniform of blue shirt, darker blue pants, and black cap, sweeps the garbage that the unceasing monsoon rain has deposited in the alley in front of the parking garage. The neighbor's dog barks to be let inside; the neighbor's persimmon tree taps at my window; rain streams down the pavement and swirls into open sewer grates.

Forty kilometers north the rain does not cease either, but the North Korean people have cut down so many trees that there are no roots to absorb the floodwaters. Torrential downpours overwhelm the shallow irrigation systems of rice terraces. The North Korean state news outlet reports housing for at least 240,000 families totally or partially destroyed, 100,000 people homeless, hundreds dead or missing, rice paddies and cornfields submerged, another harvest ruined, another food shortage of one million tons, no energy, another arduous march on the road to becoming *Kangsong Taeguk:* a strong and prosperous nation.

Monsoons billow into my dreams, blowing rain and floods into my nights. Dreams of my ex-husband, dreams of my ex-parents, dreams of abandoned relationships, lost connections, places I no longer live: my house, gutted, is only a partial skeleton of what it was, a suggestion floating in the middle of a wheat field. The roof has somehow blown off and the walls have become diagonal segments, urban rubble from a war movie. But the neatly trimmed shrubbery stands intact, marking the old boundaries. Outside the boundaries, the rain has collected and formed a little moat. Parts of rooms are still intact. My husband is still intact. He is seated in an armchair reading a newspaper in the middle of the living room. "Don't you want to salvage at least the windows and the doors so we can build a new house?" I ask him, pointing to the truck pulling away with our neighbor's woodwork, the windows and door frames filed on the flatbed like a shelf full of books. My husband is wearing slippers and reading the *St. Paul Pioneer Press.* Now I am floating far away, and there is only the sound of newspaper pages turning.

Instinct said *flee.* The meaning of memories discomforting, evidence shattered and swept up, was understood piece by logical piece. Each piece a crystal hung on a chandelier. Luminary. Paper lantern, origami, unfolding words fading in, out, float, disjoint.

A white envelope, a silver key, a leather button: I asked the piano mover to deliver them to the new owner.

Piano stripped, unhinged, legs removed. Pedal harp removed. Lid removed.

What was removed to make lighter. Wrapped in quilts.

Rattle of truck's motor

Out the door on a dolly

Out the door with your dolly

Images of departure

Images of removals

Wrapped in quilts

Stories between strangulations and suffocations uttered

Deliver us

Hands clenched, heart racing, breath coming hard—even after three years in Korea, I still wake from nightmares almost every morning, not knowing where I am, running from something invisible.

Fugitives of destruction, fugitives of failed marriages, fugitives of racism, fugitives of ourselves or of our pasts, or memories we can't remember, looking for something we can't name, not necessarily our mothers: adoptees say whatever comes to mind depending on who's asking the question, again, "How did you decide to live in Korea?"

In the summer of 2007, six hundred internationally adopted Koreans returned to Seoul from all over the world. They came from the U.S., Australia, France, Italy, Denmark, Norway, Sweden, the Netherlands,

Belgium. Most came just for vacation, but at least two hundred lived in Korea on a long-term basis. Later in the year, the second inter-Korean summit to be held since the end of the Korean War was televised, and the world saw an aging Kim Jong-il, the North Korean dictator, without his sunglasses, his trademark punk rocker hairdo thinning. It was the same year that, slightly before Christmas, a Korean adoptee was murdered by her American adoptive mother at the age of thirteen months, and another was left in foster care in Hong Kong, her Dutch parents citing cultural differences as the reason for the disruption. (They had raised the child for seven years, since infancy, and claimed she couldn't adjust to their Dutch ways. They just couldn't get her to eat the food.) Both children still had Korean citizenship, but there was more uproar from adoptees of various nationalities about the cases than from the Korean government, which should have cared the most about its citizens.

The year 2007 was also the year that I had started editing at South Korea's official news agency after deciding, more or less, to make my move to Seoul permanent. The only Korean American ever hired in that position, I was hired partly because being a native speaker of English means not being a native speaker of Korean; I got the job on the strength of my foreignness. I learned there, through editing English-language news stories, the slogan of reunification of the two separated Koreas: "One country between us."

My office was on the north side of the Han River, the old part of Seoul. I worked across the street from the Japanese Embassy, picketed every Wednesday at noon by former "comfort women" who were sent out of the country by fellow Koreans to be used as sex slaves by Japanese soldiers, and later, some say, by U.S. soldiers. Every day on my way to the office, I passed Dongnimmun, the gate of liberation, and Seodaemun Prison, where Korean freedom fighters were jailed, tortured, and executed during the thirty-five-year-long Japanese occupation. Every day on my way to work, I passed children playing in Sajik Park, where kings offered sacrifices to the gods of the land and grain.

Every day, I passed mountains where shamans bribe the dead. I passed Gyeongbok Palace, where the last queen of Korea was assassinated. In Korea—land of antiquities, modern grudges, and contemporary amnesia—we walk through history every day.

"Your history is your identity, it's what you are," Dominique had told me. He was called "Little Dominique" by the internationally adopted Koreans living in Seoul to differentiate him from the other adopted Dominiques: "Big Dominique," "Dominique-Who-Is-Visiting," and "Florida Dominic"—as if nobody had family names, or as if family names weren't worth remembering.

"Even if you think now you are a perfect woman, responsible and nice. And about love. Just ask to yourself how many times you told someone 'I love you.' You were a married woman, Jane. You will not erase the past. You have to live with," he said in French-accented English.

In Korean, he called himself *"Nappun Dominique."* Bad Dominique.

What is the shape of a marriage unraveling?

. . . the shape of my hair, dark strands carving out parentheses and asides on the floor; sound waves, the patterns of a woman's voice stating an argument against pitch silence, of those waves reconstructing space across a screen, up and down like heartbeats, the spreading of words and the silence of the house except for the chatter of the TV, the clicking of a computer keyboard, pages turning in a book; morning geometry of light inside empty wine bottles, two curled bodies sleeping in opposite directions, unclosed parentheses, holding nothing left . . .

> In the case of anxious/preoccupied patterns, the individual seems not to believe that it is obligatory to say good-bye to a "lost" attachment relationship. Rather, there is a persistent effort to recover this lost relationship, often accompanied by

intense anger and reproach expressed toward the parent. (As we noted earlier, the relationship can be "lost" in terms of the ability to provide security even in the absence of actual loss.) The inability to break free from an enmeshed dependency on an ambivalently regarded parent necessarily compromises the individual's ability to form authentic ties to new attachment figures.

. . . From the point of view of pathological mourning, the single most important cause of insecure attachment lies in the individual's inability to master the loss of a longed for but never fully experienced tender relationship to the caregiver.

—Malcolm L. West and Adrienne E. Sheldon-Keller
Patterns of Relating: An Adult Attachment Perspective

Before we had married, my husband encouraged me to patch things up with my estranged adoptive parents. Later, when my Korean mother died, he said, "You have to accept that your mother is dead."

어머니 보고싶어
Mother, I miss you.

One of the experimental monkeys was born prematurely, before the faces for the surrogate mothers had been constructed. This monkey was thus forced to live with a faceless mother whose head consisted of only a blank circle of wood. This did not seem to impede the little macaque's attachment. But after six months it was given two new cloth surrogates, one rocking and one stationary, both with completely detailed faces. "To our surprises," Harlow said, "the animal would compulsively rotate both faces 180 degrees so that it viewed only a round, smooth face and never the painted, ornamented face. Furthermore, it would do this as long as the patience of the experimenter in reorienting the faces persisted. The monkey showed no sign of fear or anxiety but showed unlimited persistence."

The monkey's indomitable preference for the familiar face to gaze at is indeed reminiscent of human love and some of its corollaries like homesickness. It also offered support for a view which Bowlby had expressed, that part of the human baby's affectional tie to the mother was its search for the mother's face.

—Robert Karen, Ph.D.
Becoming Attached: First Relationships and
How They Shape Our Capacity to Love

I read a poem about salmon, the way they struggle, the way their skin tears as they leap upstream, the way they go back for no apparent reason, they are not even starving. They are not even starving—

At work, the news stories come through the wire: *Across the world's most heavily militarized demilitarized border, they are anticipating famine . . . the children are working to farm non-arable land . . . they eat mostly cereals . . . millet and corn . . . later it is reported that the children leave school to forage for food in the mountains . . . the biggest food shortage since the 1990s is coming and the deaths will start in May if the international community doesn't act . . . South Korea says it will help if the situation is serious enough, but it's not serious enough yet . . .* the crazy uncle at the restaurant says God told him that America will attack North Korea, get out if you can, promise you will leave here . . . why do we joke that he's crazy. . . . I tell him if there is a war, I will die where I was born . . . at least I have the ending figured out . . . North Korea does not have an international adoption program and as I mentioned before, they are starving . . .

I had always imagined myself as a wife and a mother, the only options for women raised in rural Minnesota, but the reality of my marriage was a fleeting vision. At thirty-six years old I am the mother of no one, the ex-wife of a New Yorker, an ex-Korean possessing Korean language skills inferior to those of my nephew, a two-year-old Korean boy being raised by Korean parents. I am functionally illiterate, deaf, and mute in what should have been my native language in my native country.

Luckily, I had a marketable job skill when I returned to Seoul: speaking English with a standard Midwest American accent. "You speak English well! Did you study abroad?" A person who teaches English, as most adoptees do, can pay the entire month's rent by speaking English for six hours. Speak English another six hours and teachers can buy drinks for all their friends all month. An English teacher can eat out every day, and always leave food on the restaurant table. There's a center here for migrant workers and foreign brides from poor parts of Asia. They are exploited as everyone knows. South Korea has an adoption program more than fifty years old. There are real orphans and created orphans, paper sons, picture brides, imaginary orphans, foreigners born and created.

情

. . . My life of adoption and substitution, the hours of music and worthiness, and this dark scar of fear are braided together like an intricate *norigae,* its knots, its jewel, its long tassel of silk thread made to adorn a *hanbok.* Traditional jewelry, traditional clothing, traditional food— Koreans eagerly translate these cultural artifacts into souvenirs for tourists, including adopted Koreans. What was never supposed to be translated or transmitted is the peculiar Korean emotion of *han*—the deep sadness, anger, and wish for revenge whose reverse side is deep love—that filled Korean people even when they were filled with nothing else but *budae chigae*—the stew made from the discarded rations of the U.S. military. Somehow even Korean people themselves—including those adoption workers who cast out the children of the poor and the widowed—mistakenly think that what they proudly claim as five thousand years of unbroken Korean culture can be erased in one generation. As if culture doesn't come about for a reason, as if nothing is carried by the body but the hair, its color and texture wrapped around the brain, or the skin around the ribs that wrap the heart.

With my identity stripped and family removed through a perfectly legal process of paperwork, the adoption agency gave me a "clean break." The Korean government issued me a Korean travel visa for a one-way trip to America; I was never supposed to return. And I was never supposed to know the word *jeong,* that emotion unknown by individualist Western cultures, that emotion that makes Koreans say not "Korea," "Korean language," or "my mother"—but "our country," "our language," and "our mother." Now I have learned to use these words when speaking to people who insist upon my foreignness.

"*Eoneu nara eso wassayo?*" Which country do you come from?

"*Uri nara eso wassayo.*" I come from our country.

Uri, uri, we, our. Our family, our home, our culture. That feeling of jeong—in which Koreans recognize themselves and each other as Korean—binds together mother and daughter, teacher and student, friends and friends, and keeps us together as one big Korean family even when we're dining on GI trash.

But children who are sent overseas for adoption—given a chance to rise above the shameful facts of how they came to exist and an opportunity to regenerate their identities—are not supposed to know about that emotion of Korean togetherness. After all, who wants jeong with people who deserve to be purged from the nation? So the adoption agency exiled me for no crime except my birth to a battered wife, and I learned the history of my adopted American ancestors: adoptive father's ancestors lived in Young America, Minnesota, produced Minnesota's first woman pharmacist, later moved to farm on Lake Harlow, six generations now produced on that land, still living there; adoptive mother's ancestors came from Prussia six generations ago, long-documented history of intestinal disease, sometimes fatal.

I was not supposed to know the suffering of my own Korean

mother as a young woman, bearing a Japanese name not her own, chewing on a language not her-our own, her-our country filled with a foreign military, a barbed-wire gash running through the body of her-our nation, running through her-our family, her-our country now filled with another foreign military. Was never supposed to know, was never supposed to know about occupations, or her-our family for that matter, was never supposed to be involved in that . . .

−◁○▷−

I don't remember Mrs. Dunlap's face. But I remember her cat's face—its dinner-plate eyes, how it sat on the television and yowled while I waited for my sister Carol to finish her piano lesson, how from behind the closed door of the piano studio I could hear the muted *click-click* of the metronome swaying back and forth, back and forth, *largo, andante, vivace,* the measurements of time. I remember the smoke, blue-gray against the green fern wallpaper, how it haloed my sister at the end of thirty minutes, how Mrs. Dunlap and I began each lesson with an open notebook, a sharp pencil, and a fresh cigarette, my teacher's glass ashtray placed next to the highest key.

Mom had lured me into piano lessons with a question I couldn't say no to: "Do you like pushing buttons?" And then it turned out that I was actually good at piano. But Carol—she was exceedingly good. "Don't you wish you could play like that?" the relatives asked me, awed by her ability to play anything. "Beautiful Savior," "Onward, Christian Soldiers," "O Sacred Head Now Wounded": Carol could play the whole entire hymnal. Carol was so good that she surpassed her own teacher.

"I can't teach her anymore," said Mrs. Dunlap.

And so we learned that the best piano teachers are the ones you cannot have, the ones who keep a long waiting list. That's how Carol, first, and then I—after what seemed like endless waiting—came to Miss Betty M. Moss of 2222 Penn Avenue. Miss Betty M. Moss, holder of a thirty-person waiting list, professionally trained and certified by the Sherwood School of Chicago, enforcer of timed practice requirements, owner of a real grand piano. Miss Moss—*Miss* for over seventy years—who taught eighty piano students each week and who unapologetically charged a lot of good money. Always present, never sick, with a regimented, tried-and-true way of doing things, from teaching theory to motivating students with prizes, to keeping her pink settee covered in plastic, to wearing ankle-high hose underneath her slacks. When she invited her students into her kitchen for ice cream after home piano recitals, we saw that her orderly ways extended even to her kitchen: she numerically labeled Tupperware bowls and their matching lids with masking tape, filing them in her cupboards like legal documents.

I liked the comfort of the circle of keys, playing my scales in order, each major key followed by its relative minor, methodically adding and subtracting sharps and flats to step around the musical house again and again, twenty-four times, before ending up where I first began. I liked the neat division of rhythm with no remainders and no ambiguity: two eighth notes in a quarter note, two sixteenths in an eighth, two thirty-seconds in a sixteenth. Music meant order, inevitability, mathematical precision, the things we know for sure.

"You can be a Mozart specialist!" Miss Moss exclaimed. Never mind that I didn't even like Mozart: he was the musical answer to my childhood arthritis. Mozart's music does not require a large hand; the physical motions required to play Mozart are smaller in scale than those demanded from massive, romantic composers like Brahms or Rachmaninoff.

Small hands: my nemesis. Later, while in a ten-year piano-teaching career, I realized that my hands were approximately the size of an average nine-year-old's. If I had been practicing and my skin and muscles were supple, I could reach an octave, the thumb and pinkie forming a 180-degree angle. If I were not in practice, my span shrank to the width of half a key, smaller than the bare-minimum requirement for reach at the piano.

But whether because of my small hands, playing the piano too much, the weather, or genetics, the doctor could not pinpoint the reason for the pain in my hands. His clinic, just down the hill from my high school, was an old Victorian house. In the exam room (a bedroom), the doctor drew my blood, sent it to the lab for tests, read the results, wondered out loud, measured the circumference of my joints, recorded their ever-expanding dimensions, sent me to the next town for X-rays, drew more blood, wondered, wrote out prescriptions, and found out exactly how many medications I was allergic to. But despite all his poking and jabbing at my uncooperative little veins, he was never able to figure out why my knuckles were as swollen as an old woman's, why my hands hurt so badly that they woke me up at night and required soaking in hot water before I could play the piano.

With the insides of both my arms bruised dark purple and yellow, and with no further possibilities for diagnosis, the doctor recommended that I quit playing piano.

I decided to quit going to the doctor.

Although I could enjoy playing the piano for hours by myself, for my own enjoyment, playing solo piano in public was a different matter. Becoming distracted for one moment meant I might not play as well as I wanted; becoming distracted for two moments meant I might make an audible mistake. Anything more than that, and the whole enterprise could fall apart. In the worst-case scenario, the music could stop completely and I'd have to start again from a familiar section. The pianist's responsibility of keeping all the music going, all by herself, in real time, requires her to make more decisions per second than an air traffic controller.

Miss Moss's Spring Recital gave me an annual clue that I was afraid to play the piano in front of people. But in college, where I was given the opportunity to perform at least once a week and sometimes more, I discovered that I had crippling stage fright.

Piano teachers explain stage fright as a symptom of being under-prepared. The technique for getting rid of it, then, is to increase one's confidence by practicing and performing more! Musicians say that a little stage fright actually helps; the adrenaline rush enlivens the music. The worst thing in the world is an apathetic, robotic performance.

Somehow I never got my adrenaline to work for me instead of against me. My stage fright took on the physiological dimensions of a fight-or-flight response. I would have preferred flight. Before a performance, I stayed near the bathroom. During the performance, I could not stop the feeling of dread as the most difficult parts approached; I could not escape the sense that I was creating the unstoppable present, beat by beat by beat, relentless forward beats. There was the struggle to breathe, the racing heart, the merciless itch on my back, the hot, medical stage lights, the tightening forearms (are these *my* forearms?), the icy hands, the cold sweat on the keys, the racing thoughts completely unrelated to the piece at hand, the need to go to the bathroom yet again, my unanswered prayers to simply vanish from the stage, and finally the missed note, the big splat, the ear-splitting failure—and the embarrassed shuffling of the audience: rattling of programs, coughs, exhalations of disappointment, the pointlessness of finishing the wrecked piece, and finally the polite claps as I bowed, performer and audience going through the charade of having had a lovely time. Followed by punch and cake in the atrium.

It was Chopin's cruel C-sharp Minor Scherzo that really did me in: octaves, octaves, and more octaves at *presto con fuoco*—fast as hell and pants on fire. But the only fire I managed to ignite was the burning sensation creeping up my arms. By the end of college, I was at the end of my technical rope. In the artistic medium of piano performance— part athletic event, part soul work, part magic trick—I had failed. Was it because of a fundamental lack of musicality? Had I reached the limit of my natural ability? Was the filing system—key signatures, rhythms, Tupperware lids—already too ingrained? Music should make you feel intensely alive, not make you want intensely to disappear. I considered never playing again.

Yet I still loved the piano and I wanted to play it well. Most of all, I couldn't imagine life without the piano; it had been with me for so long. So I decided to make one last-ditch effort. Post–college graduation, I asked a new faculty member to take me as a private student.

Diane had graduated from the Eastman School of Music with a doctorate at the age of twenty-four; her teacher, a child prodigy, had been the youngest person ever to win the prestigious Chopin Competition in Warsaw. And *her* teacher was the great pianist Arthur Rubinstein. Diane introduced me to the recordings of Martha Argerich, who, unlike Brendel or Pollini, is not an aristocrat of the piano. She is more what people describe as "a force of nature." Though I learned later that it is futile to imitate other people—especially Argerich at the piano—her recordings showed me exactly how I wanted to play. I wanted to play with a musical imagination so strong that I could reveal passages and structures that had been hidden in music even hundreds of years old, passing the familiar melodies through my hands in effortless gestures, like great swaths of expressionist color on canvas.

I asked Diane if perhaps I should play nothing but scales and Czerny exercises for a year, but she assured me that I could learn the technique inside the music. It took a little bit of genius on her part to assign Prokofiev's *Visions Fugitives* as my first piece to study with her. With this set of twenty short, evocative, self-contained pieces that sound like musical *sijo,* Diane completely broke—and rebuilt me—as a pianist.

Underneath one of Diane's two black grand pianos in her studio, she kept a trampoline to teach the natural physicality of rhythm. To her, the impulse of music—which is both the anchor that keeps pages upon pages of black notes from skittering away in chaos underneath one's fingers, and the energy that keeps them moving always forward—was as natural as bending one's knees in response to the elastic trampoline, and the ability to divide a beat into any number of parts—four to a beat, five, or seven—was as easy as clapping one's hands. On the music desk of the same piano, she kept the scores that she was learning, and underneath the other piano, a few more. Her hands, with their slender palms, squarish nails, and fingers that seemed twice as long as mine, reminded me of the famous cast of Chopin's left hand made after his death. Her very straight back gave her a freedom of arm movement at the piano, and she zipped around the keyboard as if nothing could have been more natural, with the sense of ease and joy that comes only to born pianists.

"See—it's like a hand massage!" she said, when I finally got a small motion right. I had been moving my wrists up and down and lifting my fingers high for at least fifteen years by the time I found Diane, who taught me that wrists can turn side to side, radius over ulna. She had thrown all antiquated notions of painful and physically impossible "finger independence" out the door in favor of using the body in the way that it is already miraculously designed; hers was a completely natural and flowing technique based on rotation and weight distribution. In her hands, the gymnastics of a Chopin étude seemed like a natural consequence of possessing hands.

But building technique after breaking everything you learned before is an exercise in uncertainty, probably like learning to walk again after a horrible car accident. Take a muscular movement you've never thought about much, if at all, and suddenly think about how to do it. How do you walk? What moves first? The hip, the foot, the ankle, or the toes? How much weight on each one, and where exactly to place that weight? With which part of the finger does one touch a piano key, with how much weight from the arm, and with how much twist of the lower arm or bend of the wrist?

Playing the piano is a physical act. Out of necessity, teachers touch students, but it's not the touching in the piano lesson that makes intimacy. The intimacy of the piano lesson is built by the risk and vulnerability of the student, the willingness to make mistake after mistake, contained by the patience and guidance of the mentor. After another crash and embarrassing noise, another fight between my human body and the giant machine of the piano, Diane showed me, again and again, how to do it.

Inside the safety of her studio, with its soundproof door that shut out the judgment of others, and the promise that the next appointment would always come again in one week, Diane taught me how to use my own anatomy—the base of the thumb, the shoulder blade, the arch of the palm, the web of skin between the forefinger and the thumb. When I felt hopelessly unable to master a movement, she manipulated my body so I could experience the movement, and then do it myself, committing it to memory.

Over the course of a year, we isolated and analyzed every technical and musical challenge Prokofiev presented, sometimes studying a whole phrase, sometimes the space between two notes. Moving from the breath into the fleshy part of the fingertip, and finally the shoulder blade, Diane taught me each choreographed movement I had to make to play *Visions Fugitives*. In a way, it was paint by number. But in another way, it was a lesson in how to be free.

When I had mastered all twenty *Visions Fugitives*, I had finally learned to play the piano.

The nature of my piano experience is contained in the mundane equations of the physical world: rotation of radius and ulna, a movement calculated from the base of the thumb, force equals mass times acceleration equals *fortissimo* equals *pianissimo*. Yet the study of the piano demands understanding of both the mechanical and the spiritual. About the spiritual—I'm sure now that my piano playing ultimately faltered because of my lack of faith in big leaps. It was the reason why although I was a decent pianist, I would never be a great one. Faith in anything wasn't something I was able to achieve, either in piano lessons or in the Missouri Synod Lutheran Church, despite years of fundamentalist religious instruction and playing Sundays in church from age thirteen right through the end of Lutheran college. Instead of faith, what I learned was fear, and it had become knotted up in the piano, in my adoption, in the accoutrements of the middle-class life given to me. Adopting through Lutheran Social Services, my parents promised to raise me as a Christian, and I showed devotion to Christ, my parents, my adoption, and my church through the piano. *The Lord giveth and He taketh away* was another way of expressing my Mom's oft-repeated phrase: "Use it or lose it." The taking away is the fearful part, the part where just out of plain superstition you're too scared to ever stop practicing the piano, because, after all, this is not like riding a bicycle.

Finally, less than a year after my Korean mother died, I quit the piano. Yet because music is where I spent so many years, I return to music again to give form to experience, to make sense out of unease, dis-ease. I return to music to remember. My memories are these: the eyes of a Siamese cat, a pattern of ferns, a row of Tupperware lids, vials of blood in a line. Music is a place where we can sort out what can and cannot be saved—money, time, children, sinners. Here is a scale that weighs the love of mothers: empty your pockets before you step up. Here is luck, here is solitude, here are the cribs of an orphanage. See how they are lined up like the keys of a piano.

Chapter Two

—◄o►—

Lentamente

Here is Prokofiev. He has just completed composing *Visions Fugitives*. He is twenty-six years old.

Prokofiev is dressed in a dark suit and a clean white shirt, and it is evening. We have lit the candles on the parlor windowsills and have offered our friends tea in china cups. Now we take our seats in a half-circle around the piano. Prokofiev's hands are long and pale, his cuff links inlaid with pearl. His black shoes are shined, his feet ready at the pedals. A final cough and rustle of dresses, a clink of teacup against saucer. And then we are quiet, intent. Prokofiev lifts his hands and then allows them to fall, softly, on high white keys. The right hand voices a clear melody of single notes above the transparent chords of the left.

I let the visions float into my mind: a long, flat line. A horizon vast, wide, barren. A bump in the middle. Focus on the bump and zoom in: a man walks *lentamente,* slowly; a top crust of ice fractures beneath his steps. The collar of the man's overcoat is turned up around his face and meets the brim of his hat, the undercover cop kind, and though his tie is hidden, I know from the movies that it is striped diagonally, beige, red, and blue, and I know the kind of newspaper he carries rolled up in his hand, leather-gloved, what his wife and her apron look like, and how she's been baking all day, how his kids jump to greet him when he opens the door. And when he turns his head, I see the other thing I already know: he is white.

TRANSFORMATIONAL ÉTUDE NO. 1

Words in English

Thoughts in English

Why Korea language cannot do?

I have no thoughts in   my mother tongue

I am incapable of loving in   my mother   tongue

Division by language

Barrier

Barbed wire fence

They look for footprints in the morning

A mind violently occupied

The language of my enmity

A musician's sense of music is closely tied to color. Color has to do with the timbre of an instrument, the characteristic of a voice, or—more sensitively—the key center in which music is composed. A musician can hear the brightness of E Major (the key of "Spring" in Vivaldi's *Four Seasons*), the richness of E-flat Major (the key of Beethoven's *Eroica Symphony*), or the darkness and sadness of D Minor (the key of Mozart's *Requiem Mass*).

When I gave piano lessons to children, I tried to teach them this kind of vocabulary. I started by asking them to think in images even as they learned an aural skill. "Let's pretend that this is the sound track to your own movie. What's on the screen? Who are the people, the animals, the landscape? What are they doing?"

I learned what obsesses fourth graders: dogs. Different breeds of dogs. Dog toenails. Dog birthday parties! And stories of catastrophe: people being ejected from airplanes and landing in swimming pools, other people's fathers falling from roofs, and sled dogs that somehow get loose and devour the neighbor's herd of pet deer.

When the sound track is the opening of *Visions Fugitives*, my movie is a man walking across a plain of ice toward the horizon. He is wearing a beige, red, and blue striped tie. His wife has baked a cherry slump. His children are playing cars. One son looks like the wife, the other looks like the husband. The children are both white. The wife is white. The man is white. They are an American family, and no one disputes their Americanness.

Frog-eyed nigger-lipped Dumbo-eared chink is what my best friend called me and I laughed like I thought it was as funny as she thought it was . . . You are supposed to laugh at your best friend's jokes, right? . . . So I swallowed it whole and went back for more because out of all the girls in my grade she was the nicest to me . . . when she felt like it. And then I was a grown woman, and I wanted to make peace with my mom before I became a bride. But I mistook peace for truth, so I told her how it was growing up in that town, how profoundly painful and lonely it was in all that whiteness, and I asked her why she didn't stand up for me and she said, *So what, all kids are mean, everyone gets teased, if they didn't tease you for being Korean they would have teased you for something else, like being fat, so why do you expect special treatment?* And at that moment I knew that my white mother doesn't see me . . . doesn't see how other people see me . . . chooses to see me without my body . . . because she can make that choice . . . she can choose to live in her imagination where I am white too . . . because I am her daughter . . . and she does not see that during those eighteen years I lived in her house I was not human . . . and the day I married my white husband, I was thirty years old and I wore beautiful Korean robes and beautiful makeup, a beautiful smile . . . My hair was perfect. No one could tell me what to do . . . And underneath it all I was still a chink.

What is the point anyway of telling stories like that? Among a certain population they are terrifically banal. We who find them banal have developed our own grim humor around anecdotes like that, which often begin with "Back in the day when I was still white." We are really tired of the way other people often use words like "painful" in reference to our lives.

Common questions adoptive parents ask me: "Do you think culture camps are good?" "How do I protect my child from racists?" "Should I force her to learn Chinese?" "Will my child ever truly be mine?"

We want someone to ensure that everything will turn out right. We want to invent cures and identify preventable causes of unintended effects. We want to quantify and categorize, to formulate a repeatable experiment, to place things in logical order: one, two, three. Following. First next then finally last. Resulted in. As a consequence of.

TRANSFORMATIONAL ÉTUDE NO. 2

Made in Korea

Cheap goods

Cheap labor

Cheap womb

Cheap adoption

Cheap immigration

Cheap immigrant

Cheap yellow daughter

Honorary white almost but not quite

The following has been posited by people of color who have no problem calling themselves people of color and were probably raised by people of color and it does seems like a good idea: the center of discussion should move away from whiteness. Let's not talk about white people anymore; that is a symptom of our colonization. Let's focus on ourselves.

About itself, Korea fantasizes that it is racially homogeneous. In Korea, my family members are not people of color. They are Korean, the same way everybody they care about is also Korean. In Korea, my family members are not minorities, immigrants, or Asian Americans. In Korea, my siblings grew up surrounded by Korean people.

In Korea, I am pretty. My mother's genetic gift to me is natural *ssang kapul,* the coveted double eyelids obtainable to most only by surgery. In Korea, I am not freakishly small; I can easily find clothes that fit me. In Korea, I am an overseas Korean. I am an overseas adopted Korean. In Korea, I cannot speak Korean. In Korea, I am not a real Korean.

So tell me then, what is the nature of the place to which the discussion ought to move?

TRANSFORMATIONAL ÉTUDE NO. 3

That which expresses the inexpressible

Universal language

Music at the piano

I know the piano's history

I do not know the names of traditional Korean instruments

I do not like the sound of Korean instruments

My sadness is inexpressible

This language did not create it

This language cannot contain it

They took the child's tongue

They took the mother's eyes

You have heard that tale before. It is a common punishment.

CHANCE MUSIC FOR ADOPTEE SOLO

(Performer may play consequents in any order desired following the antecedent.)

Antecedent (Question) Phrase

How is your project of mental decolonization going?

Consequent (Answer) Phrase

1. How you give love is one thing. How you feel love is another.
2. The best piano teachers are the ones you cannot have. The best mothers. The best daughters.
3. Of all the love in the world, the love I want most is that of an aging white woman.
4. Between love and rejection lies fear.

REPERTOIRE OF DREAMS

1. Thousands of movie Indians are gathered on the prairie, on horseback, wearing buckskin clothing and headdresses. Later, Yo-Yo Ma makes a guest appearance with his cello.
2. I have done my own makeup. I have applied dark eye shadow in the creases of my eyelids. "That looks stupid," says my white friend.
3. I am in the kitchen at an enormous house party. There are only Korean people there. They are speaking Korean. *We are your extended family,* they tell me, accommodating me in English, and when I ask them their family name, it is not mine.
4. I am at an enormous picnic. There are only white people there. My friend has done my hair and makeup: she has covered my hair with a wig in a pageboy cut. The bangs

are thick and straight. She has shaved my eyebrows and drawn fake eyebrows above them. I am an old Hollywood version of Oriental, and at the end of the picnic, everyone has gone home but me.

Overheard: "Why do they keep having babies?" "They are patriarchal." "I was surprised that they love their children." "Do you want them to die in the streets?" "Nothing for her there but a life of prostitution." "They will languish in orphanages." "But I love her so much."

TAXONOMY

1. All Asian countries like each other. TRUE/FALSE
2. Korean adoptees know the particulars of Chinese adoption. TRUE/FALSE
3. An adoptee can freely move between his or her culture of origin and adopted culture. TRUE/FALSE
4. Foreign adoptees are more likely to have physical and mental problems than domestic adoptees. TRUE/FALSE
5. Foreign adoptees are more likely to excel academically than domestic adoptees. TRUE/FALSE
6. Asian American is synonymous with Asian. TRUE/FALSE

The sound of my words is a musical color. "This is the language I speak" is one color. Spoken in Korean, *This is the language I have lost* is another.

I long for questions I can answer, tasks I can accomplish.

High on the keyboard, a melody: winter horizon. A man walks across a barren plain of ice. See the color of his coat and hat, his tie and gloves, his hands, his wife, his children. Now the melody repeats, embellished by a chromatic scale, all keys and all colors spinning, tessellations of ice crystals and light. A sun dog burns in the sky. Underneath it, the man steps slowly, lentamente, this man of my imagination, this white man walking through the season of my amnesia.

Andante

Can the reportage of the senses be trusted—their synesthesia, their hybridity? All right then: back to things. Nouns. A noun is a person, place, or thing. A thing wants a form. A fairy tale is a form to describe a thing. The form possesses people: orphan, stepmother, prince. Places: a land far, far away, the Black Forest, Bethlehem. Things: a cottage, some apples, a star. And ideas: the idea of beauty, the idea of envy, the idea of possession.

Beginning, middle, and end: that is how fairy tales work. Enter the variables of person, place, or thing. Fairy tales are ready-made. Beginning: the heroine's skin is white as snow. Middle: instead of the heroine's heart, the hunter has procured words. He opens the lid of his box. Inside are all the words that cannot be translated. See how the words squirm like baby mice in a nest, how the contents of this box are proof of the hunter's success.

Orphan, stepmother, prince: in fairy tales, manipulate the variables until the good guys win. X, Y, Z: in math, manipulate the variables until the value is equal on both sides. Cross multiplication is easy because it so conveniently cancels out nearly everything. Look inside the box again. Maybe the contents are neither a nest of words nor the heart cut out of a deer. Maybe what lies inside is the heart of another mother, and maybe that's how the negative value of loss became equal on both sides.

Fairy tales are ready-made. In some versions, the queen desires to eat her daughter's vital organs with salt. A long, long time ago, this idea was not uncommon: the idea of killing and eating the object of envy so the eater could take what she wanted by absorption. The idea of beauty. Heroines are white as snow. My fingernails are chewed to the quick.

In a time very, very recently, writing teachers became pessimistic about adjectives. But without adjectives, how would we know that heroines have golden locks? How would we know that the forest is dark, that the witch is wicked, that the orphans are hungry? Orphans are always hungry. You can feed them Spam and chocolate bars and poisoned apples all day long and they'll still complain about emptiness. That's why the government manufactures cakes made of grass. The cakes have no nutritional value, but they possess a magical property that makes orphans feel full.

Is math a thing, like a chair, or an idea, like possession? In calculus, you're supposed to substitute zero for numbers approaching zero. But isn't that cheating? There is a difference between a child with an orphan visa and a child whose parents are dead. Approaching zero is not the same as zero.

This note on the piano sounds like a bell. The bell sounds like a light. The orphans follow the light. The Magi follow the Star. Eat the person you envy. Eat what you desire. My nails are chewed to the quick. The quick and the dead, we will all be judged. The body of Christ, my own body, of Orient are, star of wonder. Tears taste of salt. Myths come ready-made. They possess their own syntax. The thing that wants a form is a thing that cannot be said. The thing that wants a form eludes us even as we recite the fairy tales that never belonged to us, the fairy tales we know by heart. Say them again and again as if they will give you the things you want but do not have.

The orphan has an insatiable hunger. There is a thing inside that wants. Around the thing that wants, there is a sequence of words that tries to name the thing, the things that we do not know. We want the words in the box to stop their incessant motion and do what we tell them to do. *Sit down. Be good. No means no!* We want orphan to mean orphan, mother to mean mother, daughter to mean daughter. Nouns with no adjectives, nouns that are what we expect them to be, words that name what things really are, steady and real, solid and dependable.

Person, place, or thing: Key. Bell. Star. The last notes of Andante: a series of high Gs against the dark forest of A-flat. Listen: these sounds are the things that we cannot talk about, things that we cannot name but vaguely in metaphors, and although the end is approaching, it seems now that there is no true beginning except the one we mark officially with *Once upon a time,* and in these stories, our own stories, we are always somewhere in the middle, spinning wool or scrubbing floors, encased in a glass casket inside a cottage, or trapped on the wrong side of the kingdom, far, far away.

Allegretto

A melodeon's pumping rhythm　　mechanical tune

Chromatic means strike each key

Repeat it at the fifth　　reproduce it at the octave

Children of mysterious birth

Who were sent across oceans inside sealed papers

Who appeared, before which they had disappeared

Who encountered strangers in strange lands

Who responded to terror　　　　as if mechanical

Who repeated the terror　　　　reproduced

MASK DANCE NO. 1: THE REMOVAL OF THE HEART

At County Market, the biggest and lowest-priced grocery store within a fifty-mile radius, Mom and I are standing in line. Mom is clutching her store coupons and manufacturer coupons that she had unfiled earlier from her recipe box and its twenty or so categories: sauces, detergents, canned goods, toiletries, salad dressings, boxed cake mixes, dried and instant foods, cooking oils, chocolate chips and other baking supplies. Every week we go to three or four grocery stores to get the lowest prices, matching the coupons to the in-store specials, and I think our family is tired of eating the same cheap food, ground beef presented in different shapes, a circle being a hamburger and an oval being a hamburger steak, and not watching movies at the cinema anymore because it's too expensive and in general we are tired of being who we are: high school–educated, lower-middle-class whites, honest, good people who work hard for a living, who grow vegetables in summer, chop wood in fall, and put jam up for the winter, residents of one of the poorest counties in Minnesota with one daughter in college in Minneapolis, her tuition payment suddenly felt in the family budget, on the family dinner table. This knowledge of who we are quiets us as the checker scans each item from the Anishinaabe woman's cart in front of us and Mom looks on with envy as packages of all kinds of meat, not just hamburger, beep by: one, two, three, four, five, six . . . Then the payment comes out—paper food stamps—and the checkout girl spreads them one by one all over the stainless steel counter, in order to stamp them more easily with her heavy industrial-strength silver metal stamp—*bam bam bam bam!*—well, maybe not for ease, but humiliation. The Anishinaabe woman does not acknowledge our stares, but finishes bagging her groceries, puts them back into her cart, and wheels through the automatic door toward the parking lot.

Mom hands her coupons to the checkout girl first thing.

At the dinner table over oval-shaped ground meat that evening, Mom and Dad agree that their hard-earned tax dollars should not be spent on food stamps for lazy Indians and their screwed-up tribal elections at White Earth, couldn't ever hear the end of drunk Indians and their damn elections. "And even I can't afford to buy that much meat," added Mom. Dad is a sheet metal worker in a factory; for almost twenty years he has stood in the same place in the line riveting pieces of metal together into heating and cooling pipes. Before that he worked for the creamery delivering milk. Mom is back again at her job as an unlicensed dental hygienist and secretary in a dental office after a brief stint manufacturing potato chips on the graveyard shift at the Barrel o' Fun snack food factory.

Wait, I almost forgot the vocabulary of my hometown dialect: *Squaw.*
Prairie nigger. The hometown bumper stickers: *Save a Walleye, Kill an
Indian.*

Wait, I almost forgot: in two years the checkout girl at County Market, who took that $4.25 per hour summer job in order to save up and
buy Christmas presents for her family, and who would spread the
food stamps all over the counter for everyone to see, for everyone to
hear—*bam bam bam bam!*—would be me.

MASK DANCE NO. 2: THE REMOVAL OF THE TONGUE

Keeping a Protestant family together hinges on the beliefs that everyone is the same and nobody should be treated different and nobody
should get anything special—which is not faith in the invisible, but
invisibility.

That in senior high I had spent hours fabric-painting my denim
jacket with a globe and a row of paper dolls linking hands with the
words "Mankind Is One" emblazoned across the top I now think of
as a wonderfully beautiful, naive gesture of self-defense, just a step
up in sophistication from my first-grade defense: a green, torso-sized
schoolbag with a giant red ladybug silk-screened on it, held strategi-
cally over my face on every forty-minute bus ride to and from school,
every morning and every afternoon, long bus ride, longest part of the
day. The bold message of my schoolbag-shield: "Don't Bug Me." Mom's
insistence that I choose a new schoolbag each school year was, at the
beginning of first grade, fun, but at the beginning of second grade, a
cause for panic. "Can't I just use the same one? OK, then can't we buy
a new one that's exactly the *same*?"

You can't talk about what you don't have vocabulary for. That includes not just racial hatred but also racial friendship. So fast-forward
to high school, and there we were: a group of girls—all who just happened to be friends because of our personal qualities, like niceness—

all sporting late-1980s hairstyles and doing our best to fit in: one Nicaraguan refugee who spoke only Spanish, a product of the CIA and church rescue; one Hmong refugee who had been learning English since second grade but who still had an accent (ditto on the CIA and the church); one suspected half-Indian who knew better than to mention it; one daughter of a Filipina wife and a white GI who also knew better than to mention that; and one Korean adoptee.

MASK DANCE NO. 3: PASSING FOR WHITE

Almost thirty years after retiring the Don't Bug Me schoolbag-shield, I was invited to the opening party of a seafood restaurant in Seoul by another adoptee. The people there all had Korean faces, including a handful of Korean Americans who worked either in the American military or had some kind of business association with the military. One told me about the jet-set life that selling weapons afforded him; he was vacationing in Korea, visiting relatives, but he lived in Washington, D.C., and had just come back from Iraq. "What a fucked place!" was his entire commentary on it.

Another, a career military man high-ranking enough to be forbidden to talk about what he actually did in the military—but who was rumored to be able to both kill and skin a rabbit with a plastic straw and break a man's leg on purpose as part of his job—was doing all he could to be sent to Iraq for the first time. They hadn't let him go yet, probably because he was too high-ranking, but he wanted it. He was recently divorced. "The military has given me a good life," he said in his pack-a-day voice. "Now it's time to pay the piper."

We ate as much seafood as we could, with fins, without fins, in pancakes, in soups, alone on plates or rolling around in ceramic dishes, still in the shell. Did I say that everyone had a Korean face? There was a man there who I thought maybe was half-Korean, but he kept joking—insisting—all night, "I'm just a white guy." Late in the evening, I asked him why he kept asserting his whiteness. He told me that he had worked in the U.S. military as a translator, and he told me about the racism inside the military. "I'm really a Cherokee Indian," he said. "But it's easier to be white."

MASK DANCE NO. 4: THE PASSING OF THE BELOVED

There are some Polacks and various Scandihoovians around too, but up towards Menahga, the home of St. Urho, who fought the grasshoppers, it's mostly old Laplanders. My aunt married one, who in turn became Uncle Finlander, and their son was my cousin Shad. Half-Finlander, he was my mother's dearest nephew, the inheritor of the family skin color, eye color, good cheer, generosity. He was also the inheritor of the family illness, Crohn's disease, and a decade of that compounded with a dilapidated liver blossomed into cancer—everywhere. We could see it on his skin. He lived to the age of twenty-nine years, two months, and twenty days.

We had grown up a year and less than six miles apart. At our grandparents' dairy farm and at the homes of five sets of aunts and uncles, we shared tractor rides, pitchers of milk with the fur still on the rim, endlessly fun cardboard boxes, highest positions attainable atop haystacks, and cheese puffs served as legitimate hors d'oeuvres. Our moms made sure we also shared the chicken pox and somehow parlayed our mutual misery into a coffeecake event. Those are the days I wish I could hold on to forever, chicken pox and all. But we grew up, I in my way and Shad in his. He became the Minnesota ideal—a beer-drinking, joke-cracking, deer-hunting, truck-driving, good ol' boy. He must have been grouchy or crabby or mean some days, but I swear I never saw it. Not even once, not even when he was a kid.

I went to see him before he died. Though emaciated, gray, almost unrecognizable, he was still Shad. Still funny. Still chatty. Still concerned for other people and trying to host his own end-of-life reception from his basement bedroom. Upstairs at the dining room table, his parents recalled the people and places of his life: his childhood home and childhood friends who dressed up in suit jackets too big, his grandparents' home place with its ancient sauna and those steaming rocks, his dorm room and all the beer parties, those good buddies, those hunting weekends, those places he would never see again, that girl he would never marry.

His mother washed the body.

At Shad's funeral, his mother—my aunt—announced to everyone, "It is an absolutely glorious day to be in God's Kingdom." She was sure that God was making good on his promise of eternal life, that Shad had become an angel, and was now spending eternity playing with puppies and children. My aunt's dignity was that of a mother who had cared for a son from birth to death, who organized everything with grace—the flowers and the food, the thank-you cards and the phone calls, the payment of the bills, the cleaning of her son's room and the washing of the sheets on his bed—including the care of her normally cheery husband, whom I had never seen cry before.

We all grieved in our own ways. My cousin's girlfriend, once divorced, shook and cried, kissed Shad's cheek in the coffin, and fell limply into the arms of her girlfriends. My sister brought her two young children, who were inexperienced in funerals and who asked questions like, "Who do they bury here?" and "Why did he die?"

After the burial, we drank coffee out of Styrofoam cups and ate from paper plates with plastic sporks, affirming life on the cellular level: seven variations on Cool Whip salad, homemade pickles, buttered ham buns. I passed time with my parents. "Why'd he have to die?" they demanded, echoing their grandchildren and trying to make sense of loss, shocked in the way we are when someone dies terribly expectedly.

"He didn't need to be here anymore. He's been sick for ten years, he had enough suffering." My aunt mixed up her tenses.

"He was the son we never had." Mom and Dad repeated it all weekend. "He was the son we never had, the son we never had. We raised him like the son we never had."

"And we raised three daughters," replied my aunt, who in actuality had only one daughter, but also two Korean nieces. She squeezed my arm.

RULING LISTS "STALKERS" AS SEXUALLY DANGEROUS

St. Paul Pioneer Press
Wednesday, May 21, 2003

A person with a history of obsession that includes stalking and death threats can fall under the legal definition of a sexually dangerous person for purposes of incarceration, the Minnesota Court of Appeals ruled Thursday.

The ruling will now apply to [my stalker], now 34, whose sexually deviant behavior began when he stalked another student [me] at college in 1991, according to court papers. [My stalker] first began watching the woman undress and his obsession with her escalated until he shot at her father and was later arrested, according to court papers. Police searched his car and found a pistol, a knife, duct tape and a video camera for the planned kidnapping, rape and murder of the woman, court papers state.

Once incarcerated on assault charges, [our stalker] exhibited similar behavior with a prison guard. He refused or didn't complete sex offender treatment several times during his sentence. He was released on probation in 1997 and was allowed to leave his house to run errands. Instead, he bought a gun and set off to find the female guard.

He was arrested and, again, police found a loaded gun, a knife and duct tape in his car. Authorities also found two lists of names of prison officials, judges and others involved in his case . . .

MASK DANCE NO. 5: LITERARY PASSING

> ... *the author's presence—her or his intentions, blindness, and sight—is part of the imaginative activity.*

> *Eddy is white, and we know he is because nobody says so.*
>
> —Toni Morrison
> *Playing in the Dark: Whiteness and the Literary Imagination*

When the sheriff arrested my stalker in Becker County, four hours away from his home in the Twin Cities, they interrogated him about the burglaries of the past few weeks, as well as the shooting. The transcript of the interrogation is nine pages long and mostly has to do with where he was and when. But embedded in the middle of those questions is this exchange:

Q: *What do you have relatives up here?*

A: *I have relatives on the reservation. I've never—haven't met 'em, but I—they're up here and I am registered and I wanted—I've been . . .*

Q: *What are their names?*

A: *See, that's what I don't—I don't know. I was gonna go up there and try to find the tribal office and I ended up not doing that, but, uh, that's one thing I have never been. I'm just a quart—quarter Indian. I never been involved in that. I just— I was gonna go up there and, uhm—*

[The scenes of the Mask Dance are punctuated by music. At the end of the drama the entire village participates in music and dance.]

quarter-Indian > half-Finlander > whole Korean > family register > registered Indian > recognized as > right to call oneself > I never been involved in that > right to documentation > documents public > documents private > decisions made > people nullified > invisible colored > whiteness visible > age of stalker at time of crime = 23 > looked at me > framed in window > years since creation of White Earth = 139 > years of existence of foreign occupation of Korea = 111 > framed by fences > age of stalker at first trip to White Earth = 23 > I was just gonna go > couldn't find relatives > I'm just a quart—quarter > I'm just ad—adopted > my age at time of first trip to Korea = 22 > just went > found relatives > despite blindness > despite mind > despite loathing of self > never been involved in those Asian American organizations > where you gonna go > I never been > what must be witnessed > registered > incarcerated > I recognize you now > and what of the family you wanted > the son they never had > and what of the family you never found > never been >

These encounters.

Animato

1

There is an inner ear of imagination that transforms image into sound, and sound into image: a herd of wild Icelandic ponies galloping across a plain of twenty-four-hour daylight; a gymnast's glittering ribbon describing arcs and spirals around her tumbling body; a clock set into the hump of a golden camel. In its pulse of strike and wave of decay, the music of Prokofiev creates its own time, in layers within the same piece of music, organized by the beat, its second hand.

The inner clock of a metronomic steady beat isn't hard to develop. But the skill of expressively manipulating the beat is more difficult to learn. *Rubato,* from the Italian word *rubare,* meaning "to steal," is the musical term for this manipulation.

Rubato: to steal time.

2

Umma, my Korean mother, told me how I was born, the fifth daughter of my father, on lunar date January 24, 1972, 2:00 a.m. Outside, it was snowing; outside, I emerged from my mother's body. It was 2:00 in the morning, and my father would not let my mother into the house, and it was March 9 and it was snowing and it was dark. At the same time, it was March 8 and lunchtime in Minnesota.

When I traveled to America, I traveled backward in time, over fourteen time zones. As long as I live in Minnesota, I will be the beneficiary of fourteen more hours. Fourteen extra hours—enough to make me one day older than I officially am, fourteen hours that give me one extra day.

A mother's nakedness. The tessellated hours.

3

On summer nights, daylight saving time is one more hour saved from darkness. In spring, "spring ahead." In fall, "fall back." In Korea there is no such thing as daylight saving time.

4

I remember a song with lyrics about Judgment Day. They stick in my head, as do all the songs from my teen years, when I thought I might grow up to be a songwriter for Christian rock stars like Sandi Patty or Amy Grant.

"One more day could separate the world. One more day, and time could be no longer. What would you do if you had one more day?"

5

WIDELY ACCEPTED SPECULATIONS

"If you had not been adopted—"

"If you had stayed in Korea—"

"If you did not come to America—"

—I would have died, I would have become a prostitute, I would not have gotten an education, my growth would have been stunted, I would have been trapped in a backward society, I would have been an orphan, I would have been homeless.

My American mother believes all of the above.

In a landscape of burning whiteness, of isolation and absolutes, there are two ways to describe: Right or wrong. True or false.

Nevertheless, I tried to tell my mother about how it really was, the pleasant things and the unpleasant things, too, the vast gray area of my adoption. I tried to tell her about my Korean family, about me.

She cuts me off. "I guess I'm just a bad person," she says.

My mother is a good person. My logic is not the same as hers, but I understand hers because she raised me with it. She has to believe that treating me "as her own" (and no one else's) was absolutely, unquestionably right. Good people do what is best for their children. Good people are good mothers. Good mothers raise happy children. Good mothers never hurt their children. Good mothers are good people.

My mother feels that she has to choose between two things: her own goodness or the truth of my experience. In the end, she chooses her own goodness.

I guess I cannot fault her for that.

I also want to believe that I am good.

6

My sister Carol and I were on the phone, killing time while I waited for my first afternoon piano student and she waited for her kids to come home from school. It had been about two years since we began to talk to each other in adulthood, after a long absence.

"It's wonderful, getting to know you again," I told Carol in a fit of fondness. I was happy about the way I could instantly tell how her day was going when she picked up the phone, how I could tell whether she had been dusting her house by the state of her allergies, how I knew any number of the kind of small, inconsequential details you know about someone with whom you are intimate. And then, although it seemed risky, I told her what I had been holding back during the previous two years, those two years of listening and sharing memories, of getting to know each other's husbands and her kids, those two years into our pact to be sisters, no matter what: "It's wonderful to know you because, quite honestly," I ventured. "I don't remember growing up with you. I don't really remember you in our house."

Of course, we grew up in the same house, the three-bedroom rambler my parents built shortly after they married in 1964 and had lived in for the next forty-plus years. I had some memories of Carol—tiptoeing into her room at night to sleep next to her, the clothes she crocheted for my dolls—but for the most part, I couldn't remember her. I learned most of what I know about her in adulthood.

"Funny," Carol said. "I don't really remember you either."

During those same years, my younger sister, who grew up in Korea fourteen hours away, remembered both of us. But she remembered us simply as a story that our mother told, again and again.

7

Here is how I learned to bend time: my piano teacher turned on the metronome and asked me to play. My task was to hear the metronome and play around it, but not with it. After much practice, the metronome became a point of reference that I could touch or not touch at will, and time itself became fluid.

In modern performance practice, it is considered correct to play *rubato* with one's hands together: left- and right-hand notes line up the way the composer wrote them on the page, even though the pulse is fluid. But during the time of the great Romantic pianists, it was more fashionable to play with a slightly different pulse in each hand, to enhance the music's expression. Chopin's rubato was described as a tree in the wind; his left hand was the steady trunk and branches; his right hand glided over the sound of the left like flickering leaves.

8

A proper noun my Korean mother never spoke: "Jane."
A proper noun my American mother never spoke: "경아."

9

The tempo of a piece of music refers to its speed.
In Italian, *tempo* is the word for "time," from the Latin word *tempus.*

10

Writing books is exactly the opposite of playing the piano. When I play the piano, music frees itself from the page and lifts into life, the present. When I write, I gather up passing images and bind them to one spot. These words: past, present, future. These phrases: what might have been, what is.

11

My memories of my parents' home are strewn with dolls, mine and my mother's. In the closet next to the board games, she kept a doll she received at her bridal shower, a bride about two feet tall. As a child I couldn't understand why an adult would want to have a doll, but I suppose it was not to play with, but to reflect the bride. Later Mom began collecting decorative figurines, scouting auction sales for Hummels. On our living room end table, an old woman in a brown dress and white apron stood holding a basket full of fish. Later, an elderly couple showed up underneath the TV set. The man was standing next to the stump of a tree that he had apparently just chopped down. Then a small boy with yellow hair underneath his gray hat showed up on top of the china hutch. Then another boy appeared with yellow hair and a red bandana and a patch on his pants. They all looked like they could be the children of my parents. Later, I would marry a man who looked like he could have been the son of my parents.

At fourteen years old, it took a long time to earn enough money to buy a figurine for my mother, even an inexpensive imitation of a real Hummel. Nonetheless when the figurines of the boys my mother liked so much turned up on the clearance table at Bergen's flower shop, I bought all of them. Every one. For my mother, I lined them up on the top shelf of the china hutch, eight boys who looked like they could have been her children in different poses, fishing, running, jumping, resting, reflecting.

My blue-eyed, blond-haired mother, what I wouldn't do to be loved by you, your pale blue eyes, your flaxen hair.

12

The menu for our wedding reception was all-German: sauerbraten, Wiener schnitzel, chocolate torte with orange jelly topping. We held the celebration at the Black Forest Inn, the place where I had discovered how strong the German heritage really is in my family; the authentic German food served there is pretty much what we eat at home, if only in a slightly Americanized form: sausages, lots of casseroles, fried liver and onions, potatoes and more potatoes, meat things floating in gravy. It's as if my family enacts Germanness without even knowing it via the kitchen.

Characteristically, my parents didn't say anything about the choice of food or reception hall; I'm not sure they realized that the German reception at the Black Forest Inn was really for them, not my husband or me. One more piece fell into place when my husband and I ate there again, on a day when I was craving fried liver and sauerkraut. The Black Forest now sells T-shirts with its logo emblazoned on the back. On the front: "Non-Germans love it. Germans find it surprisingly adequate."

When I applied to Augsburg College in Minneapolis, I didn't know that the food culture off-campus would be part of my education. But the Cedar-Riverside neighborhood, of which the campus is a part, is traditionally an immigrant neighborhood, and a wealth of immigrant businesses line Cedar Avenue—including the restaurant Koreahouse.

Koreahouse is two tables wide, and as with most hole-in-the-wall restaurants, the trick is to stay focused on your food without looking at the floor or the walls. I convinced my Wisconsinite roommate to go there with me, and without knowing anything about Korean food, we randomly ordered and ate what came out of the kitchen.

I spent the rest of the afternoon sick.

But I kept going back to that Korean restaurant, even without the security of my white roommate, acclimating myself to the Korean version of sauerkraut and enjoying the presence of the owner-waiter, who I thought was Korean. He showed me how to eat my bibimbap, mixing the vegetables, barbequed meat, and raw egg together with the red pepper sauce. I made it my project to eat what I wanted to become, as if to reverse the effects of everything I had eaten before, all those pallid noodles drenched in cream of mushroom soup.

One Sunday, I decide to skip brunch in the college cafeteria and eat at Koreahouse. The restaurant was quiet, and as I ate my meal that was sure to make me sick later, the owner sat down at the table with me, a photograph in hand. In the photograph, there were a dozen men in orange jumpsuits. He pointed to himself and told me in broken English that he had been a pilot in the Vietnamese military. On one mission, he was shot down by the enemy, and everyone on the plane died in the crash except for him; he only broke his leg, but that's why he still limps on rainy days. He was taken prisoner and spent years in a forced labor camp before he walked across Cambodia to his freedom.

My response: *YOU MEAN YOU'RE NOT KOREAN?*

Tempus fugit: Time flies.

13

Maybe someday I will wake up and find myself in the right story. *Once upon a time, I was Korean.* This is a fairy tale that is never told because everything about it is completely normal and realistic. In this fairy tale, there is no magical birth, all the children are raised by their mothers, and there is no quest for what is missing. Everything is ordinary. The protagonist is a middle-class working woman, married with children, the owner of a store. She has never made love to a white man, nor does she wonder what a Korean man's body might be like. When she prepares for her wedding, she has no problem finding a little ceramic bride and groom set that looks like her and her husband, to decorate the top of her wedding cake. In this fairy tale, the protagonist's fingernails are not the stubby nails of a pianist. They are long, and manicured.

14

Nor is this music exactly a fugue. It gives the impression of a fugue, but it is only an elaborate working out of a single motive, repetition and layering, side by side, right hand first, staggered and staggering against the left, contrary motion.

15

Daylight saving time   regulation of darkness
Miscegenation   crime   theft
"Ignorance is no excuse under the law"
"What we didn't know back then"
"What we learned from them"
Friction of two things   What is between them
"What we thought was right"

What remains

16

My blue-eyed and blond-haired mother, set the kitchen clock back and behold me as I came into your life, the child of another. In our imaginations, unfettered by time, fall back and behold my friends. Let them be never abandoned in alleys or police stations, never lied to about their parentage, their cities of birth, let them never be the inheritors of the family names of orphanage directors for want of their own. Let them have real birthdays. Fall back and the gray metal adoption agency drawers full of secret files and the unspeakable names of mothers and fathers that anyone but their own children can see have no reason to be secret, fall back, and let us always be safe. Keep us from harm, for when you bend time like this, to evoke a season of finer imagining, mothers are never desperate, neither my mother with the black hair nor you, my beautiful mother with the golden hair and pale blue eyes, whom I wanted so much to love me.

—◄o►—

Set in one of the most beautiful natural landscapes in all of Minnesota, it looks like a redbrick boarding school, only with barbed wire and far more fences. It's where they incarcerate the criminals who have already served their prison sentences, but who are considered too dangerous to be released into the public. It's the repeat child molesters and the repeat rapists who've already ruined enough lives, who have no hope of rehabilitation, who end up there. My stalker—the man who had detailed to the police his elaborate plan to rape, kill, and bury me for his sexual gratification—is one of the people who ended up there. But a century ago, people were sent to the hospital for other reasons, like homosexuality, or grief from a spouse's death.

Today this place is called the "Minnesota Security Hospital" or simply "St. Peter," after the town that houses it, but in the past the people of Minnesota have known it by many names, including "the Hospital for the Dangerous Insane."

Molto Giocoso

WEDNESDAY NEWS FROM THE HOSPITAL FOR THE DANGEROUS INSANE

St. Peter, Minnesota

Wednesday, April 12, 1882

John Bloomquist of Oshawa was adjudged insane on Saturday and sent to the hospital. He lost a horse last fall and a cow this spring and it appeared to affect his mind. He thought he was going to become a beggar.

Wednesday, June 28, 1882

The Delano Eagle intimates that a young lady of Wright county was sent to the hospital at this place by the county officials of that county for the fees, and that the officers knew that the girl was not crazy. The Eagle says that the friends of the girl have written to the Superintendent Bartlett, and ascertained that the girl can go home at any time, as she is alright. If the statement of the Eagle is correct, the county officials of Wright county must be hard up for a little cash.

Wednesday, August 16, 1882

The hospital for the insane records show that in there were received at the hospital at this place 15 men and 21 women and in July there were 19 men and 9 women received, making the total for the two months 64, average 32 per month. This is above the monthly average but it certainly shows that insanity is on the increase.

Wednesday, November 8, 1882

Mr. G. B. Everett, leader of the State Hospital band, received a telegram last Thursday informing him of the sudden death of his father at West Medway, Massachusetts. Mr. Everett took the first train east and it will be some time before he returns.

Wednesday, March 28, 1883

A pleasant dance occurred on Friday evening at the upper hospital for insane. The music was furnished by T. M. Perry and his assistants. They say it is real fun to see those crazy folks dance, and we propose seeing the next performance if we can learn when it is coming off.

Con Eleganza

I dream in color, and I dream with sound track. Usually the sound track is orchestral, but sometimes it's more intimate. For instance, the sound track we are hearing now—a sliding melody, a limping rhythm, six-eight time—was recorded on a slightly out-of-tune piano. Enter a single dancer dressed in a groom's costume on one side of the body, a bride's on the other. A distinct vertical boundary separates lipstick from beard, veil from top hat, dress from tux. The dancer is awkward, contrary, a parody of something supposedly immutable: bride and groom, male and female. The dancer is spinning, black-and-white, black-and-white, a whirling dervish alone, undoubtedly animated but failing to be elegant in rented formalwear, or to be convincing in drag.

Why not split the spinning dancer. Let one dancer become two—how about John Travolta and Olivia Newton-John—and let them dance in a way that is unconfusing. Let them be the coolest dancers in the world. Let Travolta be skinny again and pumped with testosterone, and let Olivia be lustrously feminine and wide-eyed and carefree. And while the music is playing and they're dancing in the flashing red and blue lights on that linoleum-tiled floor, why not roll out a stainless steel buffet cart, VFW bingo hall–style, or better yet, why not move the dancers and the tiled floor to a real restaurant buffet with sparkling glass sneeze shields protecting the big steaming tubs of food. The beauty and mystery of buffet are the infinity of mashed potatoes and stuffing, how the handles of the serving spoons shine as they emerge from mac 'n' cheese or bread pudding, how someone has actually taken the time to make all those macaroni salads, how you can choose between the massive stump of roast beef or ham at the end of the line, and when you do, the man in the chef's hat will slice it paper-thin for you with his serrated knife and place it wherever you still have room on your plate, and if you don't have room, he'll find a place on top of your corn. As you walk back to your booth, you watch the colored tile to make sure you don't slip, and that pulls your eyes back to the other things on the floor, such as Olivia's feet, so comfortable in high heels, rhinestone ornaments sparkling above her toes, such thin and well-shaped legs peeking out from underneath the skirt of that white halter dress, such stunningly platinum blond hair throwing off light in the glow of fried chicken heating lamps. She is so beautiful that she can give her beauty away to strangers like that, recklessly, without dropping a single dance step even while waiting for ham.

Buffet is best, but Banquet TV dinner is a close second when your parents are at work. Remember to take the aluminum foil off the apple compote and stir the mashed potatoes halfway through baking. After lunch, my sister and I do the Hustle, we do the Snoopy, we draw the moss green velvet curtains in the living room and wave flashlights at each other, sing into hairbrushes and ice cream scoops. This is real disco—peppermint roll-on lip gloss, feathered hair, tank tops, jogging shorts. We wish we were as cool as our older cousins, the ones on our dad's side, whom we hardly ever see because our dads don't like each other, but who can probably dance because when we see them in pictures they are airbrushed and popular, perpetually high school seniors in corduroy blazers and baby blue turtlenecks. These are the last days of summer vacation, testing the limits of the volume on the radio, dancing, singing, reading books while snuggled into the familiar smell of the gold couch cushions, familiar sound of the electric fan, familiar afternoons when we wait for Mom and Dad to come home.

◄○►

My sixth trip to Korea in ten years. Late summer 2005, my divorce just finalized. *Hedwig and the Angry Inch* is playing in theaters—a Korean in a blond wig pretending to be a German man pretending to be a woman. It's the weekend before school starts, officially after rainy season, but still rainy—typhoon season. I am awakened by the chant of the fruit and vegetable vendor. Up and down the steep hills and alleys, the trucks drive laden with watermelon, peaches, nectarines, onions, cherry tomatoes, potatoes, yams, and intensely sweet purple grapes with skins you pop off and leave on the table. Roses are in full bloom, cosmos and black-eyed Susans line the roadsides. My neighbor grows a bush of *mugunghwa*, the national flower, and yellow and orange flowers shaped like trumpets; the tomatoes mingling with morning glories on her rooftop will soon be ripe. The fruit on the persimmon trees is hard and green; in the fall they will be squat and orange, and those who have trees growing in their courtyards will break off branches of waxy leaves hung with ripe fruit to give as gifts to friends. Later, too, pumpkins and squashes will appear on rooftops, mandarin oranges from Jeju Island will come into season, sidewalks will be covered in gingko seeds, and zucchini on the vine will inch across rooftops, power lines, telephone cables. But this is the season for harvesting red peppers and laying them out on mats to dry, spreading them in a single layer wherever there is room—in parking lots, on the pavement in front of stores, on the hoods of cars. Once every few days, a new harvest appears, and the previous day's harvest dries wrinkled and dark.

I know the alleys and the shortcuts, where each set of stairs without signage begins and ends, which subway lines are quick and which are slow, which transfers are long or short, which shops to visit to buy the few things I need to live. I know how the air quality changes in the different parts of the city, from the choking bus fumes and open sewers of Sinchon to the clean cool breezes of Cheonggye Stream, from the thick green smell that tumbles down the mountain that rises behind the Arts Center in Seochodong, the neighborhood where my mother lived until she became ill, to the incense- and lotus-blossom-scented temples scattered around the city. I know how to tell, in a city where the sky is seldom blue, what kind of gray sky means rain and what kind of gray sky means sun with smog. In the hidden parks, heather mingles with wild grasses and bamboo; the wind makes a soft hushing sound when it blows through the stands. The air buzzes with voices: crickets and cicadas, tree frogs, yellow spiders waiting in their webs for prey. I have filled my stomach with nourishing seaweed in broth, potatoes caramelized in soy sauce, legs of squid fried in onions and batter, rich

stews of vegetables and fermented bean paste, sizzling pieces of barbequed pork and greasy garlic wrapped in sesame leaves, thin slices of
beef cooked in a pot with mushrooms and yam noodles, raw tuna and
flatfish, soup made from the blood of cattle. I have eaten the leaves of
yams, shepherd's purse, wild mountain vegetables. I know the distinct,
animal flavor of this country's milk, the texture of this country's red
apples and round yellow pears. I know the taste of what comes from
this land.

Yet at night, I always dream of America.

Chapter Three

—◄o►—

Pittoresco

Heard at Inje University, at a program for adult adoptees, 2005:

"You can learn the Korean language very fast, because you are Korean."

"You are not Korean unless you can sing 'Arirang.'"

"You are a real Korean because you feel emotions like we do."

"You might not understand this movie because it has Korean emotions."

"The most important things in culture are food and language."

"Can you cook Korean food?"

"Why don't you speak Korean?"

The same continuous pattern, *ostinato* in the left hand, A E A E A E, the interval of a fifth, a rolling circle of sound, bottom to the top and back again, a wash of harmonics, this series, the piano's strings open and ringing, six beats in a measure, 123 456, count the predictable beats, a quarter note gets one beat, quarterdeck, top of the wave and back down again, movement with the pulse of water, cool salt breeze against the starboard side of a ship.

> I received a passport for foreign travel and an accompanying document to the effect that I was going abroad on an art mission and to improve my health. There was no indication as to the length of my stay. In vain did one wise friend warn me, "You are running away from history, and history will never forgive you: when you return you will not be understood."
>
> —*Autobiography of Sergei Prokofiev*

My transpacific experience mutilated: transpacific travel with the Pacific cut out. Airplanes erase the space in between, the feeling that one has traveled far. Look how quickly I can come from here to there and miss the whole ocean, the coral reefs, the whales and dolphins, the glitter of sunlight on the water, and all the things reflected in one's mind during such a long trip, during such a space of transition that I have never experienced, a space that has shrunk to imaginary.

Heard in my family:

> 1995: "Your mother wants you to learn Korean. She is too old to learn English."
>
> 1998: "Your Korean is improving. Your mother tells you to study hard."
>
> 2000: "Next time, we'll speak Korean together."
>
> 2002: "Next time, we'll speak Korean together."
>
> 2004: "Hurry and learn Korean. Study hard."
>
> 2005: "You are so smart. You can learn Korean in one month."
>
> 2006: "When are you going to learn Korean?"
>
> 2007: "Your two-year-old nephew speaks Korean better than you."

Interval: the space between.

Right hand crosses over the left, a deep bass D, followed by a shimmering chord in the right hand. Another bass D, resonant, a lush chord, lap of turquoise water, cry of seagulls, postcard images, postcard expectations.

Paper cutout of an ocean, paper cutouts of mountains. When you paint mountains, make the colors lighter as they fade into the distance. When you listen to rain, hear how the sound comes in layers, how the rain also sounds lighter and lighter gray as it fades into the distance.

Imperfection of sound. The way sound travels. Learn to listen to reflections. Hear the piano's sound returning to you, altered, from the back of the concert hall.

Your writer's voice, have you found it, have you developed it, have you changed it, lost it, have you made a political choice to write in English? Have you—

Pittoresco   picturesque
Dolcissimo   very sweetly
Pianissimo   very softly
Espressivo   expressive
Musical passages
Middle passage
Culture of passing
Exquisite displacement
What follows
Reflex of tongue and thought

Another word with no English equivalent: 아쉽다, *ashuipda,* verb, meaning to deeply, passionately want to have or to do something, but to not be able to fulfill that desire. Dictionary example: 네게 아쉬운 것이 없도록 해주겠다. *Nege ashuiungoshi eopdolok haejugetda.* You shall want for nothing.

Biblical example: the Lord is my shepherd, I shall not want.

Commodo

Sino-Korean syllables pronounced 문 *(mun):*
　門: gate; door entrance; opening
　們: a plural marker for persons
　問: ask = mouth + door
　聞: hear = ear + door
　悶: agonize = heart behind a door

I had fallen in love with the man whom I would later marry for simple, ordinary reasons. Because he called me every weekday at exactly 5:55 p.m. Because he placed his cheek exactly on the right spot, in the curve of my neck. Because he made me coffee and always had a carton of half-and-half in his refrigerator. Because we could talk about classical music together, but he was also a certified car mechanic. Because he made me comfortable.

He was from Long Island, a born and bred New Yorker, the kind who rarely goes into "the city," has never seen the Statue of Liberty, calls the subway "the train." He's the kind of New Yorker with Italian steprelatives who call pizza "pie," spaghetti sauce "gravy," and believe in incorruptible bodies.

Having grown up near Flushing, Mark was also around a lot of Koreans in childhood and later attended college with Korean musicians in Queens. At the beginning of our relationship, I actually thought, *Wow, you know more about Koreans than I do!* Which was probably true. But being around people doesn't make you one of them; it only makes you a spectator. After all, he never turned Italian on the inside, either, his own ethnic mix being German and English—incidentally or not, the exact same mix as my adoptive father.

Although love is supposed to conquer all, our marriage showed signs of being conquered right away. I asked my Korean family to attend our wedding, but it was too hard for them to get a visa from the U.S. after 9/11, so they stayed in Korea. My elder sister sent us wedding geese and traditional Korean clothing instead. The day of the wedding, there was a whiteout snowstorm, so none of the rural Minnesota relatives who had planned to drive to the Twin Cities that day could make it; only my parents and my sister and her husband and kids attended, along with a handful of the New York Italian relatives who had flown in the day before the storm. Mark—who had been raised sometimes Anglican, sometimes Jewish, and sometimes Roman Catholic—and I had decided to marry in a Unitarian church. The pastor requested that we write our own vows, which despite all our hodgepodge efforts resounded with none of the wisdom of the ages that young couples ought to get when embarking upon something as serious as marriage. Because it was impossible to find a cake top featuring a miniature white groom with a miniature yellow bride, our wedding cake was topped by two white plastic doves. I will now admit that because there were no Korean people around to show me how to wear my little Korean wedding hat, I inadvertently pinned it to my hair backward and that's why I'm still too embarrassed to show my Korean family those photos. I forced my husband to shove his body into the traditional Korean wedding clothes my sister had sent, and, like all tourists, he looked misplaced and awkward in them. He hated the idea of wearing pink silk pants.

So that is how we entered into our marriage: in a way that felt slightly fraudulent, ignorant of what interracial or even intercultural marriage means, with no role models for a marriage that could accommodate both my growing identification with Korea and Mark's growing rootedness in Minnesota, which was more comfortable for him than New York. Phenotypically as white as they come, he loved Minnesota partly because he blended in there so well; there are so few short, dark southern Italians like his stepfamily living there.

One step away from his mother's family, my husband remembered the guinea jokes he heard when his father married his third wife. But three's a charm and my father-in-law, a Vietnam vet who hadn't slept well since all those nights on border patrol, probably just told everyone to mind their own damn business. I wish I could have done the same when it came to my own marriage. But my marriage was not a German English American man/Italian American woman thing.

The criticisms that I encountered just for being married to a white man were leveled not by white people, but solely by Asian Americans. In their arguments, any kind of Asian is better than a white guy, although I am quite sure my Korean mother would have picked white over Japanese any day, if it came down to it; my mother was never Asian American, after all. I should have said that, but that's not really the issue. The issue was that those daily attacks were just one more stressor on top of all the other stressors of marriage, and I was already lonely and insecure. My husband was the silent provider type with the emphasis on silent. Now I know that he couldn't have done anything to defend us against the racial hate of the people who were supposed to be my own anyway. Defending myself, my choices, my experiences— that has always been my job.

Unfortunately, those who voiced their opinions about my inter-racial marriage weren't able to articulate themselves well enough for me to understand why Asian Americans get so upset about the high rate of marriage of Asian women to white men. To me, it just sounded like hateful ranting about who is entitled to own Asian American wom-en's bodies, why some Asian American guys can't get dates, or why the best revenge for an Asian American guy is to fuck a white woman. Only later, in Seoul, did my friend Jae-dal teach me to count the steps between myself as the wife of a white man and other Korean women, an arrangement like that of his divorced parents. Count: one step away from a Korean American woman married to a white man, one more or the same step away from a Korean wife with an American soldier hus-band. Another step away from a war bride. Another step: war booty.

Step: camptown prostitute. Step: comfort woman. Step again: comfort child.

But what was more immediately pressing than criticism from strangers or my being Asian American or his being white was that every day people have to eat. People can fall in love over a series of dinners. They can fall out of love the same way.

Because I loved him, I cooked. At first, my husband tried to please me and choked down whatever I placed in front of him. But soon he began to pick the golden raisins out of my sauces, refused to eat the mushrooms, wouldn't taste eggplant. Then he changed his policy of picking the undesirable things out: he couldn't eat anything contaminated by the juices or flavors of certain foods. Finally he added a layer of more complex rules: some methods of cooking certain foods were acceptable, but others were not. For instance, tomato sauce was fine, but tomato chunks were not. Peanuts were edible if they were pulverized into creamy peanut butter, but peanuts could not be eaten in chunky peanut butter, and certainly not by themselves, roasted. Conversely, he would eat cashews roasted whole, but not as cashew butter. Some perfectly delicious foods that were fine separately could not be eaten in combination: he would eat cabbage or beets, but not cabbage and beets. Chopped celery could occur in tuna salad to be eaten with a fork but not in tuna salad that was to be eaten in sandwiches. Some things he liked in small quantities but not more and certainly not reheated the next day. And so on. I taped a flowchart to the refrigerator.

Because he loved me, he bought me a little Japanese dog to keep me company while he was away at work. I cooked during the day and in the evenings, the dog got fat on my miscalculations. The vet said to stop feeding the dog people food.

I wanted to pack Mark's lunches, but he insisted on going out for lunch. He was not hungry when he came home from work in the evening. Late at night, finally hungry, he ate cold restaurant leftovers out of

Styrofoam containers. In the mornings I begged him to take a home-made roll to eat on the way to work, but he said he didn't have time and he didn't like the walnuts in the rolls anyway. I was left standing in the middle of the kitchen in my hot mitts and apron while the dog ate reduced-calorie kibble.

To compensate for not feeding the dog people-grade food, I allowed the dog to sleep in the bed with us. The dog found a favorite spot each night squarely between us. I spooned with the snoring dog; my husband slept flat on his back with a Breathe Right strip affixed to his nose.

Because he loved me, my husband bought a house. He made the offer before I even saw it, simply because I don't care about houses. He chose it with his friend, a licensed contractor who moved into the basement rent-free in exchange for helping my husband work on the house.

Then Mark countered my compulsive cooking with compulsive building. You know how it is when you peel something back and discover that a little facelift won't do because something structural is rotten and you have to redo the entire thing? Mark nearly gutted the house. He built a whole new porch, put on a new roof, new siding, new windows.

Because he loved me, he spent all his free time constructing and destructing with his friend. Because he loved me, he encouraged me to be independent and do my own thing. But all I wanted was for someone to sit down at the table and eat what I cooked.

His best friend, the contractor in the basement, ate.

We went through the motions of listening and of talking. We searched for genuine feelings that didn't have to be interpreted, ways of giving love and feeling loved that matched, a straight heart connection. We wanted to make things better. We wanted to not be lonely.

My husband was a fan of alcoholic beverages, cable TV, and mass-market paperbacks. I developed a taste for alcohol and cable TV, but not the mass-market paperbacks, though I tried. He had recommended an author of political thrillers and suspense to me, "a great writer," he said. I found the book on his shelf and opened it to a random page. I read about a girl named Ming with amber skin and slanted eyes. Of course her name was Ming, like a decorative vase. Of course she was quivering, but unable to suppress her lust for the American officer. Of course, when I asked about it, my husband said that he only buys that author's books for the political plots. Just for the articles, as they say.

Ironically, he would usually brush my hand away. "Later tonight," he would say. Later tonight he would say, "Maybe tomorrow morning." Yesterday and tomorrow slid around on the slick ice of time, colliding with each other like an army of identical soldiers falling down.

I remembered that once he had made time for me, conjuring it from air in unbroken circles, the hands of the clock cycling from acute to obtuse and back again. Then, how many decorative calendars later?—twelve pages of wild pintos, twelve pages of ballerinas, and twelve Monet gardens, a dozen each of all beautiful things—my calendars were discarded and the effects of housewifery lined my hands like tiny Western towns: roads, railroads, electric lines, things that swing in the wind.

We tried to make my Trip Number Five just another trip to Korea, me traveling alone to study the Korean language for four months. Though we had already talked about divorce, it wasn't supposed to turn into that. We thought we would "put our relationship on ice" and just resume things four months later, mistakenly thinking that relationships can stop changing. How deluded: at that point, I already knew that relationships never stop, not even with people you don't even talk with anymore, not even with people who are dead. Koreans, who renew their relationships with the dead every year with *chesa* ceremonies, know this well. Death is nothing. It is just about what you can see and what you can't see. Our ancestors come to visit every year when we lay out the feast table. We close the doors and they come to eat and drink, and then we open the doors when they've had enough, and they leave. Never let a spirit go hungry on the anniversary of its body's passing.

But the living need daily maintenance. Although I was the one who went halfway across the world, I wanted to be married and I wanted to feel connected, so it was me who ended up complaining about all the missed phone appointments, the absence of letters and packages I wanted him to send. It was me who craved romantic letters saying how much he missed me. He sent me a few e-mails with some links to light stores, asking which light fixtures I preferred for the outside of the house. Vinyl siding, exterior lighting, the roof, the gutters— I grew to hate Home Depot.

We had always agreed that an affair would be the end of our marriage. So I knew exactly what I was doing when I had an affair with a Korean Danish adoptee. I was getting divorced. Later the adoptee told me that I had used him. It was mutual use.

We were in love with Korea, not each other. It was the small enjoyments I fell in love with, small enjoyments I had never experienced and never would experience with my husband, like bags of mandarin oranges bought out of the back of a truck on the street, the fun of love motels, the fun of walking through Seoul completely unnoticed by others, and not noticing and remarking, as my husband had, upon other people as if they are Japanime characters, or about how short they are.

The Dane had introduced me to the Korean public bath. We went there to be in the coed sauna, but it was the women-only bath that I really loved. I loved it because I had never really seen Korean bodies before. Women and children walked around shamelessly naked and soaked their skin into softness in the same hot, bubbling bathtubs spiked with mineral salts or green tea. In another section of the bathhouse, on low plastic stools in front of faucets and mirrors, women washed their hair, applied facial masks, and scrubbed themselves and each other. With a little heat and friction, the skin rubs off in gray rolls, revealing a whole new layer of soft skin underneath. I saw Korean children who were lucky enough to keep their own Korean mothers, both adolescent girls who closely resembled their mothers and young children still carrying the bruiselike spots on their lower backs that most East Asian children have when they are born, and that fade with age. Their mothers still bore the brown stretch marks of childbearing and the scars of cesarean sections. How I envied those mothers, those children.

Inside the bathhouse, the Danish adoptee and I after three decades finally learned about bodies like ours, what other kids learn from their parents at home and in high school locker rooms. In the end it was clear that we were a poor match, but what we gave each other was an adult love of our bodies that our Western upbringings had taught us only to racialize. And we gave each other the courage to stay in Korea.

I called my husband and asked, again, for a divorce. The answer, again, was "No."

When I returned to St. Paul after five months at Inje University in Korea—the length of time for a legal separation in Minnesota—my husband met me at the airport with a dozen red roses.

My favorite flower is the stargazer lily . . .

Is it that nothing is ever good enough for me, that I can't feel love even if it's given to me, or that I just noticed that at certain times the small courtesies really matter—the remembering of the favorite flower, the courtesy of not putting empty food containers back into the refrigerator, or of listening now, in the present, instead of answering, "We'll cross that bridge when we come to it"? So many times I was already on that tired old imaginary bridge that I would never cross, toes wrapped around the railing and ready to jump. Then I was in the water and I was drowning.

Two years after our divorce, I learned that the qualities that first drew me to Mark and what were ultimately so maddening about him were, of course, the very same things: his slowness, his firm and decided rootedness in a place, his unwavering physical reliability. I knew when he would materialize at home by walking in through that back door after work, every day, at the same time. The dog knew. The piano students knew. The neighbors knew. After two years in Korea in the midst of adoptees—whose solution to intimacy, so dearly desired and feared, is so often to say *I love you* and then cut loose and run—I appreciated that when planning a visit to the U.S. again to finalize our divorce, I knew that Mark would be in exactly the same place where I had last seen him in St. Paul, Minnesota.

Therapy was my idea for the first two years of marriage, and became his idea after I asked for a divorce. At our first and only session, the counselor talked to me for a few minutes first, then turned to my husband and said, "Can you accept that your marriage is over? If you don't let this woman go, she will turn into a tiger."

Mark wrote the therapist a check for a hundred dollars and then we went out for a drink.

We spent five years together. I never hated him. I just thought, Wouldn't life be easier for both of us if we didn't have to fight about sleeping on the floor or eating rice more than once a week? I thought, Wouldn't it be great for him if he could just find someone who really cares about outdoor light fixtures, who would be happy to live forever in Minnesota, and who wasn't always yearning to move somewhere else to be around more Korean people? Someone who wanted to share his home? I thought, Wouldn't he be a lot happier with a nice white lady, preferably one who wants to spend all her time at Home Depot choosing paint?

So was it egg or Twinkie on my face when he told me that his primary emotional support during our separation was a Korean American woman whom he had met on the Internet? Later, he found a Chinese American girlfriend. Could it have been a coincidence, just someone he randomly met through work connections? How is it that my white husband had the ability to socialize with far more Asian people in Minnesota than I ever had? Was it just that he wasn't scared of them, the way I was? That he had nothing to risk by letting multiculturalism into his life?

He said it didn't matter whether his new girlfriend was Korean or Chinese. It didn't matter that I'm Korean, it didn't matter to his girlfriend, it didn't matter to him, it never mattered to anyone, only to me. We are just people, he said, we are *just people* . . .

If I were white, my husband and I might still be together, working out the ordinary conflicts of marriage: money, sex, kids. I might still be keeping up the beautiful illusion of the world as a level playing field, a place where all people get to make meaningful, personal, individual choices for the benefit of themselves and their families: a full buffet of choices for transparent, neutral, race-free people who take on cultures and countries as hobbies or intellectual interests. I would most likely be interested in Japan or China, not Korea, if I were literally white.

Yet despite the way my honorary and learned whiteness failed me, failed my marriage, failed my husband—the same way the same whiteness failed my adoptive parents and their parenthood—I truly loved my husband. Or, I loved him as much as I am able to love anyone. He was my chosen husband, after all. Yet I wonder if he chose *me*, specifically, or if I was merely interchangeable with any other Asian bride, as I had been interchangeable with any other Asian child available for adoption.

We are all human. We are just people. Yes, I have just wanted to be just a person. And I have spent my entire life recovering my humanity.

Divorce papers

Foreigner resident papers

Paper bride

Paper counting marker

Paper culture

Paper cut upon the finger

Blade upon the tongue

Blade on the heel

What sex gets you

What whiteness gets you

Gift culture   Theft culture

Chapter Four

Allegretto Tranquillo

MASTER OF THE MASTER CLASS: *Well, that was a fine, mostly convincing performance. Thank you. Well done, young lady. Now, I hear that you have a little bit of a problem at the piano. No doubt you've encountered this problem before. Hold up your hands. Show the audience. Those are tiny hands!! But Myra Hess could do it and so can you.* [Audience chuckles.] *How far can you reach comfortably? Just barely an octave? OK, so here Prokofiev requires you to play a harmonic interval right at the opening that is physically impossible for you to reach—a tenth—so what are you going to do?—No, don't do it that way because your teacher told you to! Try some things out. Figure out what's going to work best for you, see what you like. I think you have three options: roll it, revoice it, or omit notes. In any case, the goal is to compensate for your limitation. Hide it if you can. Just fake it! I'm an inner voices man myself, so I think I'd revoice it. So then the question is, how? Where are you going to omit a note that should be there, and substitute another note that's not supposed to be there? But of course whatever you do it's not going to sound exactly as Prokofiev intended, and you'd probably get into trouble for it in a contest situation. They'll make you pay in accuracy points! And you're going to pay in either nuance, harmony, or time. Try not to pay in style!* [Audience chuckles.] *But it's too bad about this piece and you—you don't have any other choice but to rearrange this thing a little bit, do you, young lady? But you could just drop the whole thing— have you thought about that? You don't have to play the whole* Visions Fugitives. *You can pick a set of eight or so—it's rarely performed in its entirety anyway—but if you decide to perform this one you have some tough choices to make to compensate for those little hands . . . You might try some exercises to stretch your span as long as you're at it . . .*

The infamous hand injury of Robert Schumann has been attributed to the use of a mechanical hand-stretching device. Although the exact cause of the injury is disputed, it is agreed that his weakened left hand forced him to give up his dream of being a virtuoso pianist. He became a composer instead (and died in 1856 in the insane asylum where he had been committed two years prior, after trying to drown himself in the Rhine River).

Naturally, avoidance of hand injuries is a primary concern among pianists. Some pianists have even taken out insurance policies on their hands. However, it remains interesting to see how the unfortunate wounded compensate for their handicap in a two-handed world.

Ensurance exercise. Perform a cost-benefit analysis on the following scenarios. Define what is "benefit" and "cost" for all parties involved. Quantify risk. Consider how the injured can be compensated. Calculate the human costs. Name the beneficiaries. Find out who pays and how. Consider what compensation seeks to hide.

SCENARIOS

1. If your value in society depended on having children, but you were unable to produce them yourself, would you adopt children? YES/NO

2. If you wanted a healthy white infant but there were none available, would you adopt a nonwhite infant? YES/NO How dark can you go? _____

3. If you wanted a healthy white infant but there were none available, would you adopt a white child over the age of 5? YES/NO

4. If you knew that your adopted daughter would eventually leave you and go back to where she came from, would you adopt her anyway? YES/NO

5. If several of your extended family members were opposed to the adoption of a nonwhite child, would you go through with the adoption? YES/NO

6. Is it worth it for social workers who are doing home studies to investigate people living in the community (e.g., teachers, neighbors, etc.)? YES/NO
How about extended family members? YES/NO

7. If, in every family, the chances of molestation rise when there is a male nonrelative living with the family, should you consider a legal adoptive father a relative or nonrelative? RELATIVE/NONRELATIVE
After how long? _____

8. If an adopted daughter is being molested, should you preserve the daughter or her adoptive family? DAUGHTER/FAMILY

9. If you were a country that calls itself a shrimp between whales, should you allow foreign soldiers on your soil? YES/NO

10. If you were poor, would you allow your daughter to marry a foreign soldier if it helped you economically? YES/NO

11. Should you appease foreign powers by giving humans as gifts? Would you offer prostitutes for their military? HUMAN GIFT: YES/NO
MILITARIZED PROSTITUTION: YES/NO

12. If foreign allies helped save you from communism, should you send your children to those same allies later? YES/NO For how long? < 50 YEARS/> 50 YEARS
Under what kind of trade agreement?

13. If your marriage to a white man doesn't work out, should you stick with it anyway, just to spite all the Asian Americans who called you a cracker-chasing bitch? YES/NO

14. What kind of crime, if any, is it for an infertile white mother to mutilate the hair of her adopted daughters whether Black (Jezebel) or Asian (Dragon Lady)?
NOT A CRIME/CRIME OF _____

15. If someone almost raped and killed a woman, should the victim forgive the criminal? YES/NO
After how long? _____
Should the state forgive/release? YES/NO
After how long? _____

—◦—

"You said there are at least two hundred adoptees living in Seoul? I feel great here. Everyone is completely crazy."

—An adoptee less than a week into his first visit to Korea,
eating grilled pork belly and drinking soju

Wednesday, June 28, 1882

Even after the North Wing of the hospital is completed, it is going to be a question what to do with the crazy people at the rate they are coming here of late.

MANUAL OF INDUSTRIAL AND OCCUPATIONAL THERAPY
STATE HOSPITAL, ST. PETER, MINNESOTA

XI. Physical Factors

In assigning patients to jobs or tasks in a mental institution, careful consideration must be given to physical limitations. Does the assignment require some or all of the following?

1. Walking	9. Crouching	17. Pulling
2. Jumping	10. Kneeling	18. Fingering
3. Running	11. Sitting	19. Feeling
4. Balancing	12. Reaching	20. Talking
5. Climbing	13. Lifting	21. Hearing
6. Standing	14. Carrying	22. Seeing
7. Turning	15. Throwing	23. Speed in Working
8. Stooping	16. Pushing	

Remove "다" from the infinitive verb and add "기" to the verb stem to form the gerund.

Examples:
    writing = 쓰기
    reading = 읽기
    listening = 듣기

Translate into Korean: walking, jumping, running, talking, feeling . . .

SUBSTITUTION DRILL

The private adoption of a healthy white American infant can cost over $50,000. This being the case, would you like to substitute a child from another country?

Examples

1. Would you like a child from <u>Russia</u>?
2. Would you like a child from <u>China</u>?
3. Would you like a child from <u>Guatemala</u>?

Now make your own sentences with a conversation partner:
Would you like a child from _____?

LET'S GO TO THE MARKET!

Examples

1. _____ *won eochi juseyo.* Give me _____ *won* worth.
2. *Kkakka juseyo!* Give me a discount!
3. *Sigan eopseoyo.* I don't have time.
4. *Bballi haejuseyo.* Do it fast.

Now negotiate your preferred price and time frame.

ADDITIONAL TOPICS FOR CONVERSATION PRACTICE:

(Grammar hint: Attach (으)면 to the verb stem to create a conditional sentence.)

1. If you knew your infant son would grow up to be a criminal, and would be permanently institutionalized from the age of 22, would you have the child anyway?

2. If you knew your child was not capable of loving you back, would you still adopt her?

3. If you could recognize a filthy fucking gook in white pajamas as a human being, would you still shoot him?

4. If you could recognize a child's mother as a human being, would you still think of taking her child from her as a charitable act?

5. If you knew the true nature of desperation, would you still use the word "choice" as a synonym for the relinquishment or abandonment of a child?

6. If you knew your survival depended on it, would you hide your heart's limitation?

Extra Credit

Write a five-paragraph essay on the word "good." Write about what it means to be a "good" mother, husband, daughter, or student. What are "good works"? Do not use other adjectives to define "good." Your essay must have an introduction, a body, and a conclusion. Make an outline before you start. Write in pencil.

> *Living in Paris does not make one a Parisian.*
> —Sergei Prokofiev (European in Russia, Russian in Europe)

There was no other time in my life that I could have just walked away from everything so easily. My Korean family had wanted me to live in Korea before, when my mother was dying from cancer, but I couldn't or didn't want to figure out how to get rid of all my things. But a divorce from my husband, who had decided to keep the house, meant that I could just leave everything.

So I brought only the important things with me to Korea. One suitcase and two boxes. Family photos both kinds, twenty-seven books, two pens, clothes. A Polaroid of my stalker, the bars of incarceration behind him. In the report it was written that he masturbated while looking at a female guard. Maybe while he thought of killing. The photos my Korean mother never took . . . where do uncreated memories go?

Here is a Polaroid of my Lutheran baptism two weeks after my arrival in America, but a year before I was legally adopted. It was five years before I became an American citizen, two months after the agency recorded that I had been sent to the Netherlands, and four years before my agency recorded that I had acquired Dutch citizenship. During this time of suspension, see how I struggle against my mother, pushing her away although she tries to hold me tightly against her chest. See how happy she is, almost delirious, not noticing that as a baby, I had rejected my own adoption. I think of what she must look like in the present, though I haven't seen her for years, her disappointment now the exact inverse of her happiness then. Even now, half a world away, I think of her and her disappointment, of my stalker and his mother's disappointment because he also has a mother, and the disappointment and long emptiness of my Korean mother. See how we did everything the best we could, look at all the things that failed to make us full, everything we failed to know.

◄○►

Because collective knowledge and memory had been suppressed over the generations, lone individuals endured the repercussions of violence. When the truth and reconciliation work began fifty years after the massacres, South Korean workers excavated sealed mines, caves, and miles-long trenches to count the bodies of suspected communists who were executed by South Koreans operating under U.S. military rule even before the Korean War started. Many of the executed were illiterate peasants who didn't even know what communism was. Some were children. To count the dead, they say, is impossible; they think there could have been one hundred to two hundred thousand executed without trial, but we may never know the exact number.

As U.S. documents were declassified, the reason behind the air strike on civilians huddling underneath a railroad bridge at Nogunri became clear: the U.S. Army in Korea had a policy of strafing all civilian refugee parties approaching U.S. positions. Colonel Turner C. Rogers of the U.S. Air Force wrote a memo to General Edward J. Timberlake, saying, "It is not understood why the army is not . . . shooting them as they come through if they desire such action." His argument was that aircraft could be used for targets more valuable than civilians.

This kind of thing, we now call "mass civilian sacrifice."

These American idioms are common in conversation, but avoid in writing:

1. Bite the bullet.
2. I'm sweating bullets.
3. It's hotter than a pistol.
4. She's the bomb.
5. I bombed the test.
6. Stick to your guns.
7. With guns a-blazing.
8. Fired up.
9. Shoot up.
10. Shoot!

A few days before I left the U.S. for the last time, there was a message on my answering machine, like one last parting gift from the county Victims and Witnesses Office. I always held my breath until I had listened to the whole thing. It was good news that time: another appeal was successfully deflected, meaning the state of Minnesota would incarcerate my stalker a little longer in St. Peter, Minnesota, at the state security hospital.

My stalker has spent his entire adult life in prison. I have spent my entire adult life getting back to Korea. I placed an ocean, a continent, half a world, and hundred-year-old newspaper clippings between me and my stalker, and from that distance, it seems I have found some compassion for him. But I wonder if I could find compassion for him living in the same state, in the same city? What if I were with him in the same room, at the same time? My breath comes short again. Reminding myself of the safety of a vast distance, I piece together my own memories and imagine some for him. I imagine we both long for a home.

Amazing what we remember, amazing what we forget. What is fragmentary is shattered is too many people I know who cannot remember exactly what happened, is too many people with whole sections of their lives missing. My adoptive mother is also included in this tally, her father accused in whispers of robbing his daughters in some perverse way never fully detailed. My adoptive mother, who was able to recall her own childhood only in bits and pieces, turned a blind eye to my sister when the thief tried to rob his oldest granddaughter on her birthday, in her bedroom.

Umma—my mother whom I love simply because you are my mother, because when I came to Korea you slept next to me and held my hand, you fed me, you washed me, you were not afraid of my body— I was never angry toward you until I tried to live in Korea. Umma, you gave away three children—my sister and me to Americans, our brother you left on the farm with his grandmother. Even our youngest sister asks, long after your death, "Why did you have to do that?"

In Korea, I started to understand the logic of the society that would not help our family, though I tried not to believe it myself: If parents fall so low that they would even give their own children away, why should anyone else help them? Why should anyone care about people like that?

I guess, Umma, the kind of mother who would do such a thing is a mother like you, a mother who would never understand how much of her child she destroyed in trying to save her. So I told the truth about my life only after you died, because even though I needed you so desperately, you needed even more for me to say that in the end, everything turned out fine. How could you have accepted forgiveness from a person as broken as I?

My body survived, that's true. I ate well. But so much of me, Umma, didn't survive. When I came to Korea to live, I could measure exactly how much had been not lost—but methodically destroyed.

The destruction of the identities and histories of the adoptees wasn't at all personal. It was just methodical. Any Korean family with a bit of bad luck—an overwhelming hospital bill, too many kids to feed, a drinking problem in the family—was vulnerable to adoption. Our Korean mothers did not understand that international adoption wasn't a really long homestay: go, eat well, study hard, and come back later. They didn't know that adoption would erase the people who we once were so completely, so irrevocably. Our adoptions would take our language, our culture, our families, our names, our birth dates, our citizenship, and our identities in a perfectly legal process. And the world would view it as charitable and ethical.

One cannot live in Seoul as an adoptee for long without noticing that something is terribly wrong. Of the about two hundred adoptees who live in Korea long-term, there is an overrepresentation of adoptees who have been reunited with their families. Those adoptees who have been reunited with their families know exactly how they came to be adopted, and usually, the story their Korean families tell is not the same story that the agency told their adoptive parents at the time of adoption.

I didn't even know how much I had been misrepresented to my adoptive parents, even years after I was reunited and learned my Korean mother's side of the story. That's because my adoptive parents would not give me my whole adoption file. What they gave me was only a skeleton set of papers: the one-way travel visa from Korea, the birth certificate fabricated in Minnesota, my baptismal certificate, etc. Although I felt that all the papers were rightfully mine, I had already been reunited, so I never felt it was important to go to my agency and get them.

However, after living in Korea for two years, I had to renew my visa, and therefore I had to get the papers. It was then that I learned exactly how methodically my history and that of my sister had been destroyed, and how badly we had been misrepresented to our adoptive parents.

I called the agency to get my orphan *hojuk*—the legal Korean family registry that records births, deaths, changes of residences, ancestral hometowns, marriages, and divorces. I already had my family's hojuk. Though all adoptees have an orphan hojuk, which is used to facilitate their adoptions by officially making them into orphans, I didn't think I needed mine because I had my real hojuk: my mother, when she was dying, had instructed my sister to go to the city office and get a copy of our family's hojuk for me. It was my mother's way of proving to me that I had never been erased from either my family or Korea.

But my birthday on my family hojuk, which I had used to get the visa in the first place, did not match the birthday on my passport. This was a fact that the Korean Embassy in Chicago, which had issued me my visa, had overlooked. But the immigration officers in Seoul noticed. In order to get my birthdays to match, I could either go to Korean court to change my birthday on my family registry, or get a copy of my orphan hojuk. Not wanting to change my birthday on my family hojuk, which I viewed as the only thing my father ever gave me, besides my life, I decided to get a copy of my orphan hojuk to settle my visa problem.

To summarize the chicken-and-egg situation, I would never have needed that piece of Korean documentation if I had not already decided to live in Korea, and therefore have need of the visa. If I had not had a reason to contact the Korean agency for that one document, they would never have offered to send me the rest of my file. And they wouldn't have sent me the rest of my file if they hadn't already had the family's permission to give it to me. Getting my family's permission was predicated on already having found them.

The agency sent documents in English, Chinese, and Korean. The English-language papers were papers I had seen maybe once in my life, but I had forgotten the contents; my American parents had refused to give me a copy, and so had the American adoption agency, citing the privacy of my American parents.

Being able to read my records was also predicated on having lived in Korea long enough to read enough Korean and Chinese with a dictionary, and then having access to Koreans who could confirm my translation.

In the small packet of old papers that the agency sent me, they included one that had been newly made so I could reconcile the "facts" on my orphan hojuk with my current U.S. passport. This new paper declared that I had been sent to the U.S.—as opposed to what had been recorded at the adoption agency in 1972. The adoption agency recorded that I had been sent to the Netherlands. In 1976, they recorded that I had been naturalized as a Dutch citizen.

The English-language records that were sent to my American parents claimed that my mother was unmarried, that she and my father just lived together, and that she had abandoned the family shortly after my birth. Yet my mother had told me that she took me to the orphanage to escape my father's violence, and on our family hojuk, the legal document, it is registered that she and my father had been married for almost four years before my birth.

My adoption was perfectly legal. All the right papers had been filled in. All the right information had been fabricated. The papers became the official reality.

If my mother hadn't found me first, only a few months after I was sent to the U.S., I am sure that I would never have searched. I would have believed that I had been abandoned by a single mother. I would have believed that my ancestral home was Naju in the southern part of South Korea—not a place called Onyang. I would have believed that I was born on March 8, 1972. I would have believed that no one had bothered to give me a name with Chinese characters. My story would have been just like the stories of so many other adoptees, who are still searching.

The true story, unencumbered by the forms that make adoptions legal and possible—that I had a family, that my mother desperately wanted me and that she loved me, that my name came from my father, not orphanage workers, and that my father later regretted the violence that he brought upon his family, which ended in my adoption—could be revealed only thirty-four years later, by a series of flukes and uncommon circumstances.

Perhaps to live in Korea for more than two years and to be reunited with one's family is special, but among those of us who have been reunited and can either communicate in Korean or have found an impartial person who will translate for us, it is common knowledge that as a general practice, we were misrepresented to our adoptive parents: Korean mothers were represented as single mothers when they were actually married to the fathers; siblings were excluded from the social histories; health histories were changed; names, birth dates, and places of birth changed. As the adoptees have located their Korean parents, some of them have found more egregious abuses: children were switched for others who were scheduled to be adopted, but who for some reason couldn't go on the scheduled day (the white adoptive parents couldn't see the difference between the child they got and the child whose photos were sent to them); Korean parents who either lost their children or put them in orphanages on a temporary basis were not allowed to take their children back later (they were told the children were not there or had died, when in reality they had been selected for international adoption); children were sent to orphanages and then overseas without the permission of their mothers.

Why had the adoption agencies done this? One can speculate on the many reasons, but what is certain is that pretty much nobody wants to adopt a child who comes from an intact family with married parents. Nobody wants to adopt a child who has been taken from her mother and whose mother is desperately searching for her. People want real orphans, not kids whose parents have put them in an orphanage on a temporary basis as an emergency measure while the family recovers from a crisis.

Although the stories in our community of misrepresentations, kidnapping, child switching, and forged records were common, they were anecdotal. So in 2007, a small group of adoptees, Korean nationals, and I started to document the abuses. Naming our group Truth and Reconciliation for the Adoption Community of Korea (TRACK) and acting on behalf of ourselves as adoptees, our Korean families, and our adoptive parents, we brought a few cases of ourselves and our friends to the Anti-Corruption and Civil Rights Commission of Korea.

The initial investigation, conducted by the social welfare branch of the commission, was not as rigorous as we would have liked. Nevertheless, we managed to officially document the information that the agencies gave on some of the issues that we brought up. That was important because we moved the information from the anecdotal to the official.

Regarding the rights of adoptees to access their own information, one agency said that it would only give it without the birth parents' permission if the adoptee "desperately wants" it. (They did not tell how to show desperation.) Regarding two cases in which children were sent away for adoption without the mother's consent, the agencies said that yes, it was true that that happened, but at the time there was no law specifically against the practice. On another two cases where the birth mother and father claimed that the children were taken by the paternal grandmother and given away without their knowledge, the agency only stated, as it did in its records, that the children were "abandoned" and that the agency had a legal right to create new identities for them. The dubious relinquishment records of me and my sister, who was relinquished separately, were excused with the statement "Our country didn't care so much about records at that time." The representation of us as children of a single mother who abandoned us was explained as a "mistranslation." The lack of a Chinese name on my records, as well as the right birth date or hometown, they blamed on my parents for having given wrong information. And regarding my Dutch citizenship—they blamed that on the city government. They said that four girls with my name were sent for adoption at the same time: one to the Netherlands, one to Denmark, and two to the U.S. There were so many of us that they just mixed us up. I suspect that it's not impossible that Jeong Kyong-ah, born on March 8, 1972, had been promised to four different families. One family got the real Jeong Kyong-ah. The other three got different baby girls whose adoptive parents never realized that they were not the same baby in the picture, and now those girls are women who have scanty paperwork and who think they're me.

These cases are viewed as rare by the general public and also by the adoption agencies. These cases of kidnapping, forgery, and child switching are seen as a few mistakes among thousands of ethical cases processed by South Korea, just a little "collateral damage." "Mistakes were made" and there is nothing to be done about these kidnappings or forgeries now, the agencies say. The adoptees are told to just "move on" by people who must think that if something wrong continues for long enough, it eventually becomes right. Remembering, after all, dredges up the past and provides numerous opportunities to reframe family separations as something other than charitable.

It is estimated that around two hundred thousand children were sent out of South Korea for adoption, but we will never really know. Many were sent without being recorded. To count us exactly is impossible. This expulsion of children, as if we had done something to deserve it, is also a kind of "mass civilian sacrifice."

But I am still alive. My face, reflected in the window of the Seoul subway car, is still the face I was born with, still a Korean face, an unbroken mask. Remembering not to speak, I ride the subway at night, crisscrossing a metropolis of twenty million people living in layers. I ride underground, over the Han River, next to highways jammed with traffic, sometimes riding to get somewhere, sometimes riding just for the sake of motion, the train rocking me to sleep; other times standing to see my own ghostly reflection in the glass doors, bisected by highways and bridges slicing through my legs, the fluorescent night lights of tall empty office buildings streaking across my chest. The salarymen in black suits and white shirts have gone home, and so have the shoe-shine men who gather the shoes of the office workers every morning, blackening them in a small room in the basement by the elevator, and bringing them back to their owners' desks by lunchtime. The cleaning women have finished sorting paper cups and plastic bottles and cutting bars of soap in half; the car wash women of company parking lots have wrung out their rags and hung them to dry. Atop neighboring office buildings, insects have finished their cross-pollination of flowers and grasses of rooftop gardens, the ecology of connectivity working even in such a hypermodern country as this—each city connected by bus, train, or airplane; each neighborhood of each city connected by bus or subway; and this, the subway of Seoul, being one of the world's busiest, cheapest, and most efficient in the world, its train cars, where every night I ride, some of the cleanest in the world, its shining windows a mirrored reality in which my reflected body is slivered into parts, to match the way my life, my mind, has been. Yet despite the catharsis of watching cars and trains rush through my body without pause, despite the possibility expressed in the vibration of the floor (there is not much between the floor and the tracks below), and despite the adoptee who, one year ago, jumped from a tall building, and how we adoptees in Seoul, who are all in various degrees of suiciding our Western lives, talk about him often (we are never surprised by an adoptee death, nor do we work very hard at trying to convince our friends to stay alive)—despite all these abandonments, all these tiny annihilations—I want to live. Despite everything they took away, despite that I am lost and alone, despite that so many times I have been close to death, I want to live.

Wednesday, August 29, 1883

Report has it that the State Hospital band has disbanded. We hope it is only a temporary disband for they furnish good music. Brace up gentlemen!

The image of my final American departure is my black grand piano being carried out the front door by three men, its lid, legs, and pedals removed and wrapped in quilts.

A day later, there was no room for a piano in my small *gositel* room in Seoul. Gositels are buildings with shared bathrooms and kitchens, and small sleeping rooms rented on a short-term basis by Korean students cramming for exams, foreign students, and Korean workers who have just moved. It is housing for people in transition. If I lay on the floor and extended my arms and legs, I could touch the walls in both directions. There was a narrow bed, a desk, a closet wide enough to hold ten garments, a desk that extended over the foot of the bed. If I kept my room tidy, there was enough floor space to do sit-ups and push-ups. The muscles in my hands atrophied to those of a typist.

I received my first job offer through an adopted friend. The job was to do what most American adoptees living in Korea do: teach English.

Afternoons after school, I rode the subway from Sinchon to Dongdaemun, transferred to the blue line, and rode south to Ichon-dong in the Yongsan district. In the subway I counted the number of young women with slim legs, bleached and permed hair, blue contacts, unnaturally high noses, eyelid surgery, invisible scars, and the number of magazines with women on the covers who were no longer recognizable as Korean. I counted the number of advertisements featuring Daniel Henney, a TV and movie star in Korea. With a white American father and a Korean adoptee mother, he looks mostly Korean, but his Western features cut through just enough to make him an upgraded Korean, a whitened-up Korean. Of course, he speaks great English. "Dan-i-el!" middle school girls in blue uniforms and kneesocks screamed, rushing to his giant image in subway corridors to kiss the poster, trying to embrace his two-dimensional image. Korean, only upgraded, Korean, but new and improved, he had advertised for the international adoption agency that sent his mother to Michigan. I weighed the seduction of whiteness, of empire, and measured my own complicity.

Erasure as passing

Erasure as job skill

Erasure as survival

Erasure as economic development

Does anyone remember how we came to be prosperous? Not in a straight line from American-style war to American-style democracy, but a Korean-style path—make it up as you go along—over thirty years of military dictatorships and how many hours of female sweatshop labor later—where do you think babies come from anyway . . .

The Yongsan district is easy to find on a map. Just locate the blank spot in the very center of Seoul, in the bend of the Han River. For more than a century, that place bereft of civilian streets has been in continuous use by foreign militaries—first Japan, and then the U.S.

In Yongsan, the Americans have made their own Little America: beige stucco housing reminiscent of a U.S. suburb, front lawns, quiet streets, half-alive shrubbery, sports fields, picnic tables, outdoor barbeque grills, public schools, a public library with books in English, AA meetings, Taco Bell. The military camptown called Itaewon—where the soldiers and English teachers go to find local girls, and vice versa—flanks the base on the northeast side. Kitty-corner from Itaewon, on the southwest side, is the upscale Korean neighborhood of Ichon-dong.

Low-flying choppers heading toward base skim the rooftops of apartment high-rises in Ichon-dong, where the streets are some of the cleanest and widest in Seoul. BMWs and Lexus SUVs are parked in rows outside new buildings, foreign restaurants. On the ten-minute walk from the subway station to the *hagwon* where I taught English, it was my habit to stop at the 7-Eleven for a Diet Coke, and on my way home after work, I stopped at Lucy's Pie Kitchen, named after Lucille

Ball, for a piece of the only real American pie available in Seoul—high crusts and thick slabs of filling—apple, French chocolate, grasshopper.

My students at the hagwon in that prime location all had native-speaker abilities or near-native-speaker abilities. They attended private schools in Seoul, taught in English, that cost about twenty thousand American dollars a year. Besides the tuition, which tops the average Korean's yearly income, the ticket into those schools is a foreign pass-port. On introductions day I learned that nearly all the sixth graders of that hagwon, with their ethnic Korean faces, were born in the U.S. and are therefore American citizens, that their fathers were the most powerful businessmen in Korea, CEOs of computer companies and entertainment industries, and that nearly all the students planned to go to Harvard or Yale; they already carried pencils and T-shirts embla-zoned with Ivy League logos. When I told them that I went to school in America, they gasped. I must be really rich. My parents must be really powerful. Transnational transcultural transplanted me, I traded in three degrees of separation in this small gossipy rural village of forty-eight million people that is Korea for six degrees of glorious, spacious sepa-ration in America. I separated. I escaped. I shine with good luck. I was, at first glance, the person my students wanted to be.

I didn't tell them that whereas their parents chose U.S. citizenship for them because they could pay for it and that's how their futures were secured for them through emigration before they were even born, my mother chose my emigration out of sheer desperation, that if she had had any help at all, she would have chosen to keep me with her, that she had no idea we would be separated for twenty-three years, that inter-national adoption is not some kind of extended study-abroad program. I didn't tell them that the Korean economy is built on my back, my mother's back, that I am the expendable of Korea who can pass as one of its elite in a school that hires primarily Korean American teachers from Harvard and MIT, that the only thing Korea gave my mother was an infinite capacity to suffer. My fluent English is worth everything, my broken Korean worth nothing. All I have to offer is my English, my occupation. When my students asked me to speak Korean, I made emergency evasive maneuvers—they pay me to speak English, right?

Toward the middle of the semester, my students taught me a new twist on an old homework excuse: "My maid threw it away."

Bewitching, bedeviling seduction of whiteness: I would never have guessed that the alliance of Gwyneth Paltrow and Daniel Henney could sell so many products to Korean people. They sell the hope of becoming a transnational: a person who habitually drinks wine, eats cheese, sleeps in a bed, and speaks English; a person who is white, American, and wealthy—not yellow, foreign, and the owner of a liquor store, a convenience store, or a produce stand, whose wife is degraded into doing the nails of real Americans in a nail salon, who has thrown away his own life and status for the sake of his children, who raise themselves while their parents work sixteen-hour days, and who become doctors and lawyers if things work out the way they were planned. But if the emigration to America produced not only opportunity-laden English speakers for children, but Westerners as well, then the kids might turn out rebellious and lazy, go to unprestigious colleges, be unable to converse fluently in Korean even though the parents are ironically unable to converse fluently in English, and finally end up back in Korea, unmarried, teaching English, perhaps fist-fighting with adoptees in the streets.

Ridiculosamente

What They Call It:

Korea

hanguk

한국

韓 國

Beautifully-shining-by-the-morning-sun Country

U.S.A.

miguk
미국
美國

Beautiful Country

England

yeongguk
영국
英國

Superior Country

English

yeongeoh

영어

英語

Superior Language

Con Vivacità

My cousin, whom I've never met, graduated at the top of his class from Korea's most elite university, Seoul National. The first time I talked to him he said, "Hello. I want to go to America. Help me."

I explained the difference between adoptees and other Korean immigrants to him, why I have no Korean immigrant network in Flushing, Texas, L.A., or Atlanta to receive and help him. I don't even go to church. Somehow I don't think he understood because a few months later, his younger brother asked, "When are you going to America?"

"Maybe in a few years. I like living here."

"When are you going to America?"

I thought maybe my construction was too complex, so I simplified my grammar: "Never."

"Why?"

"I just spent thirty-three years there."

(Pause.)

"When are you going to America? I want to go to America. I want to study in America. I failed TOEFL test. *Nu-naaaa,*" he whines, insisting upon my Americanness, "teach me En-gu-lish-ee!"

Later he calls me to tell me he's passed the dreaded Test of English as a Foreign Language and has decided to do his undergrad work all over again in the U.S. so he can get really good grades. He wants to visit New York, California, Texas, and Minnesota to look at campuses. I let him know I'm going to San Francisco on a short visit soon.

"Where?"

"San Francisco."

"Where?"

"San Francisco."

"Where?"

"Sahn Peu-lahn-shi-seu-ko."

Ahh . . . !

It has been explained to me that Korea is too competitive, so Koreans have to go abroad. They say there are so many smart people in Korea but not enough universities—or at least there are only three schools in the three top schools. It's true that even the people who work at McDonald's are somewhat bilingual. At McDonald's, Korean people have to use English because so many foreigners eat there, but Koreans also have to take job interviews in English, even if they will never actually use English in their jobs.

"*Unni,* how can I make my English as good as yours?" my Korean friend asked, dead set on a good job and forgetting for a moment exactly how my English pronunciation became so spectacular (even though she calls me "sister"), all the up and down inflections in all the right places. Even though most Koreans can't tell an American accent from a New Zealander accent from a Norwegian accent, much less American regional differences, speaking with an American accent is imperative.

Koreans lump the adoptees together with the foreign brides and migrant workers under the theme of "multiculturalism," which in Korea seems to mean encouraging everyone to be as superficially Korean as possible (e.g., eat Korean food, cook Korean food, marry Koreans and worry about your mixed-race kids later, do Korean rituals for Korean ancestors). To me this seems completely the opposite of multicultural. But I guess they didn't ask me. However, people hired as native English speakers, such as me, should also take note that It Could Be Worse, which is demonstrated by the fact that the touristy *Lonely Planet* guidebooks so many of us carry have distinctly different useful phrases than, say, *Korean for Migrant Workers:*

> When will you pay my back wages?
> *Millin imgeum-eun eonje jusilgeomnikka?*
> 밀린 임금은 언제 주실 겁니까?

> I cannot wait any longer.
> *Deo isang gidaril su eopsseumnida.*
> 더 이상 기다릴 수 없습니다.

I have to send money to my family.
Gajok-ege doneul buchyeoya hamnida.
가족에게 돈을 부쳐야 합니다.

I can survive only if I get paid for my work, although I understand you are having difficulties.
Sajangnimdo himdeusigetjjiman jeodo ireul hago doneul badaya sal suga isseumnida.
사장님도 힘드시겠지만 저도 일을 하고 돈을 받아야 살 수가 있습니다.

I want to leave this company because I was beaten.
Pongyeogeul danghaeseo ihoesareul tteonago sipsseumnida.
폭력을 당해서 이 회사를 떠나고 싶습니다.

I've lost a lot of blood.
Pireul mani heullyeosseoyo.
피를 많이 흘렸어요.

Could I please have my passport back?
Je yeokkwoneul dollyeo-juseyo?
제 여권을 돌려주세요?

Those useful phrases are to be differentiated from the useful phrases of the U.S. military:

Have you seen communists?
Kongsangoon bwasoyo?
공산군 봤어요?

Draw a sketch map.
Yakdo guryojooseyo.
약도 그려주세요.

Can we hide here?
Yogiseo soomulsooeeseoyo?
여기서 숨을 수 있어요?

Submit to search!
Tamsaeke unghae!
탐색에 응해!

Do not resist!
Banhanghajeema!
반항하지마!

Where are the rocket launchers?
Rakaet balsagee odee eesoyo?
라캣 발사기 어디 있어요?

We came to help.
Dowa jooreo waseoyo.
도와 주러 왔어요.

I have invisible superhero powers. I see white people, but they don't see me. In markets, I can stand right next to them, completely invading their space, and they keep rattling on and on in their English conversations as if I'm not there. If I'm holding the cheese, crackers, and dried fish tray at a party, I suddenly become visible, and then I can amaze them by asking in my impeccable accent, "WOULD YOU LIKE AN HORS D'OEUVRE?"

I am giver and destroyer. On the subway, when white Americans speaking in that loud American way sit down in seats reserved for the elderly, pregnant, and handicapped, I don my superhero avenger cape: "EXCUSE ME, LADIES, BUT DID YOU KNOW THAT THESE SPOTS ARE RESERVED FOR THE ELDERLY, PREGNANT, AND HANDICAPPED?"

For my non-English-speaking benefit, their English comes out melted: "We know. We'll move. If old person. Ask."

Sometimes, instead of the superhero cape, I wear the Korean beggar-hawker permacostume. When looking for the Hannam Foreigner Supermarket, located near the place of my birth, which is now a rich neighborhood of embassy housing and foreigner apartment buildings, I got off the subway at the right stop, and then proceeded to walk around lost for an hour and a half before finally giving up and walking back to the station. But as I waited for the train at the platform, I saw a white lady approaching! Surely she will know how to get to the supermarket! Hey, lady-who-looks-like-Mom! Help!

I approached her as she came up the stairs. "Excuse me—"

She lowered her chin to her chest, put her eyes to the ground, and waved me off, walking away as fast as she could. Yet, desperate for real cheese, like gorgonzola—not oily Korean imitations of American cheese slices coated in plastic—I followed her down the platform. "Excuse me, do you know where—"

Of course, my pursuit of her only made things worse and she was nearly running by the time I gave up on cheese.

My Hannam Supermarket story was funny enough to be worthy of retelling. It passed from me to my younger sister to my brother and elder sister. I asked my elder sister what she would have done in the same situation, and as the words left my mouth, I realized that there were two obvious reasons why she would never be in that situation in the first place. First, she hates stinky cheese. Second, she never talks to foreigners (with the exception of her two sisters who were sent to the U.S. for adoption, sort of in a tragic fluke). She doesn't even talk to foreigners when they visit her electronics store and are perfectly willing to buy a large appliance like a refrigerator from her. There are usually two or three U.S. military men there whenever I visit her, and they inevitably look around and then leave. These days there are more of them because the U.S. military is pulling out of the Yongsan district (where I was born, where the supermarket is now, and where my family lived for years), to expand its base in my sister's city. My sister says that every day, she can hear the construction on the base as they prepare for the military's big move from our old neighborhood. She doesn't want to live next to the military—our lives have already been spent in its proximity. But now her children are in school and she has built her business there in that city. What can she do but keep living side by side with the military, in the country that Koreans, among themselves, still insist upon calling "our country"?

Wait a minute. This is not what transnationalism is supposed to look like.

In this era of "goose daddies"—fathers who fly overseas once or twice a year to visit their wives and children living in the West, whom they support with the money they earn in Korea—transnationalism is supposed to look like privilege. Bilingual, bicultural children who grow up in the West have a better chance of distinguishing themselves from the millions of other Koreans who also want to get into the same universities and who are competing for the same jobs. Even for middle-class families, whose fathers are called "penguin daddies" because they can't afford to fly overseas, transnationalism is supposed to be an escape from the broken public education system of Korea. Wives who live overseas with the children can escape the duties of a daughter-in-law—a life of servitude under an embittered mother-in-law who, after a lifetime of being servile herself, gets to sit back and cash in on the labor of another woman. Transnationalism is supposed to look like choices, is supposed to look like breaking boundaries, is supposed to look like freedom.

Transnationalism is not supposed to look like sisters trying to rebuild their relationship after being unwillingly separated, families struggling to talk to each other, shopkeepers tired of foreign militarization, or ethnic Koreans asking white people for directions right in the middle of Seoul, a city where the elite and the very lowest of society are thrown together because of a common language.

In a country where "American" is used synonymously with "white," my inability to speak fluent Korean combined with my inability to be white is a deformity. I am a sort of monster, a mix of the familiar with the terribly unexpected, like a fish with a human face or a chicken that barks.

"Your pronunciation is strange."

"Oh, you're not Korean. But your face looks like Korean."

"What country are you from?"

"Japanese? Chinese?"

"America? Where are you really from?"

"Sayonara!"

All this while I'm trying to speak Korean.

Meanwhile, the praise Koreans lavish upon white people who are trying to speak Korean brings my tentative speech to a screeching halt. The same low level of proficiency that is considered a great accomplishment for a white person is just more proof of defectiveness in an adoptee. I remember how my husband stumbled through Korea on our honeymoon, murdering *"Annyeonghaseyo!"* "Hi!" to everyone's delight. "You speak Korean well!" they said, adding, "You look like a movie star." He didn't look like a movie star; he was just white.

But the most humiliating situation of all is when I am with my adopted friends in a restaurant, speaking English comfortably, and suddenly a white man speaking perfect Korean comes in and sits next to us. Without saying anything, we adoptees silently agree that we will not speak another word throughout the whole dinner.

Three years into my life in Korea, the presence of white expats would bring up in me emotions of familiarity and repulsion, and the presence of Koreans a mix of comfort and fear.

Assai Moderato

I don't know why I think I can find all the answers in music. Music, with its consequent and antecedent phrases, only raises questions that it can answer itself, like picking a fight you know you can win. Music bends time and I'm not sure that's helpful. Doing that just makes you think of things you might have already forgotten for a good reason.

So let's break it down to numbers.

The devil is a half step away from perfect. The devil's interval, the tritone, lives exactly in the middle of an octave, six notes in symmetry on either side of it. Such bedevilment this dissonance gave Western ears that it was banned in the church. Centuries after the church stopped controlling all the music, Prokofiev worked out his own problems of tension and release, of dissonance and harmony—of the tritone and the intervals called perfect.

Even to twenty-first-century ears, Prokofiev's music is sometimes too modern. What we really want are cadences. We want sequences that are orderly, that tell us where we are, where we have been, and what's coming up around the corner. But even if a composer doesn't write an easy ending, you still have to play his notes. You have to make a resolution where it seems like there is none; you have to find the piece's inner logic. You may use dynamics, a gesture, or an emotion to find the pattern. You may have to create a logic or story of your own. But in any case, if you want to play music, you had better learn to make sense out of it, these extremes.

Chapter Five

—◄o►—

Korea: World's thirteenth-largest economy.
Korea: Supplier of 167,000–200,000 children to the West, depending on who's counting.
"5.6 million overseas Koreans: We are togethering!"
"Korea.net: always by your side."

In mixed martial arts fighting, the person who controls the timing wins the match. They begin standing. At first, my friend Jae-dal dances the rhythm with the other fighter, feet, hands, and then he breaks the rhythm, gets his arm underneath the other fighter's and throws his weight to the side, unbalancing his opponent. He presses his torso against the other man's, holding him to the mat. The man on the bottom tries to lift with his legs; they are bent. The struggle is muscled, slow, crushing.

One father's hand is big enough to hold a blanket over a baby's face, the other is big enough to restrain the torso and arms. But I suppose my legs were still moving. I imagine this scene from childhood but of course there is no sound, blanket over nose and mouth.

Jae-dal said, *I could feel his elbow coming out of the joint, tearing the tendons, and he started screaming so I let him go, could you hear him?* No, we couldn't, we were too far away, way back there in the audience. *The ref should have stopped the fight! I wanted him to stop it.* You have to explain these rules to me. *He should have stopped it before the other guy got too hurt. Instead he restarted it from the feet and I got pounded and the other guy finished with two broken arms. Stupid. He should have stopped it.* I don't know these rules of fighting, Jae-dal. I agree, though, he let you fight too long, your male bodies entwined.

Making love in Seoul, slow struggle of bodies, my lover asks me not to write about him, so I take him out of this picture and it is my body alone in this space, moving slowly, the bent legs, the careful timing, the control of erotic thought.

Making love in Seoul, it's in Itaewon, the home of Hooker Hill, the English bookstores, the African American barbershops, the African and Muslim markets. It's where good Korean girls don't go at night, where foreigners smoke *shisha,* where American GIs go to pick up Korean girls standing in low and narrow doorways looking tired through their heavy makeup. In shop windows they display clothes for women who work in sequins, feathers, straps, fringes, colors too bright even for Korea. Inside the shops they sell lingerie that good Korean women would be ashamed to wear. In Itaewon I feel like a woman because I am afraid, and I stop walking to let a man walk in front of me instead of behind me, a little crime prevention, and in the English bookstore I feel the eyes of white men on me and I hear their conversations, and then I feel the fear that comes from hearing men lower their voices so you can't hear anything except one remarking, in your direction, "But that would be prostitution," as if it mattered in this neighborhood. In bars lit with dim blue lights, behind scarves hanging in door frames, it's the English teachers, the rice queens and the lesbians, the cross-dressers and transvestites, the prostitutes, the military men, the illegal workers—people like these, either foreign or defective, and me, inside this Itaewon apartment, with my invisible lover.

Particles of speech

Particles of grief

Free-floating and disrupting, corrupting

The sex of my American mother and father: so quiet as to be unnoticeable, or perhaps nonexistent. Too much energy exists between a woman's legs and it must be controlled. Turn pleasure energy directly into mothering energy, be the kind of woman who marries, martyrs, bakes cakes, skips the violence—

My lover says, *I slept with a lot of women just to sleep with them. Men can do that.* Doesn't he know that women can do that too, that a woman's loneliness can be as penetrating as a man's, that a woman can fill herself with man after man, easily, wake up the next morning feeling hollow, so easily, can do that . . .

Who attempts to get what she wants with sex. Who can use it or hide it. Who dresses modestly in long knit skirts and modest colors but wears thigh-high stockings underneath to meet diplomats at cocktail parties, smiling and bowing next to the ice sculpture—

– Had you any idea that the pissing boy is the symbol of Belgium?

– In fact, I didn't—Wow—Isn't the food delicious? What is it we're celebrating?

. . . and they chat about culture and politics while her lover's semen slips into her panties, the kind of panties good Korean girls would never mistake for their own in dormitory laundry rooms . . .

Before my friend Jae-dal's mixed martial arts fight, other friends ask if I have moral qualms about paying money to see men fight. In some other context, maybe. But Jae-dal is my friend, and I know why he fights. My friend is the son of an American GI and a Korean woman. He teaches me a new word in Korean: *kijichon,* camptown. He teaches me who works there, what they have to do; what their mixed-blooded children, when they grow into adults, have to do.

In the street, Jae-dal reads as a foreigner, an ambiguous foreigner. People think perhaps he's Middle Eastern, half-black, maybe white, but definitely not Korean. On the streets, we're stopped by a grandmother who asks if we're married. "There they go, policing my sexuality," he says. When the real police come out in the parks at night, he covers his face with the hood of his sweatshirt. In restaurants, people ask him if he is able to eat spicy Korean food. When we try to cut through a parking lot, we are reprimanded by the attendant. In these scenes of authority, he hides his face and I keep my mouth shut. In this way, we pass.

Jae-dal, you are the son of a white man, and I am the daughter of a white man. We are Americans living in Korea. Your father an American soldier, my mother's first husband a Korean soldier, a war that we never lived through but that marks us, that we can neither remember nor forget. We are Koreans whose mothers denied us the chance to be Korean. The night of your fight, I was afraid of you, not because of your bloodied face or the other man's dangling arms, but because inside the ring I could see how much you are like me—that we both carry an emotion so deep, so full of love, that its frustration can be expressed only through violence. Inside uri nara, our country, your face is unrecognizable, though your speech is close to perfect. Inside uri nara, my face is recognizable, my tongue shattered. Our country, our symmetry, Jae-dal, Kyong-ah.

Allegretto

The orphan has an insatiable hunger. The bride turned into a wife. The wife will turn into a tiger. The woman swallowed the orphan, the wife, and the tiger. With the orphan, the wife, and the tiger inside her, the woman boards a ship. Together they sail through the paper ocean. They go to a land far, far away to eat sausages of blood and salted liver. In plastic tents underneath bare lightbulbs they gorge themselves on whole eggs, fishcakes and fish broth, purple-black blood sausages, slices of gray liver, and coarse salt. A warning is heard throughout the land: blood sausages cause blindness. Dumplings are made of Chinese trash. Cabbages crawl with the eggs of insects. Eels are shot through with poison. Bags of shrimp chips contain rats' heads. No matter. The woman, the orphan, the wife, and the tiger keep eating. They eat and they eat, they eat everything they can, even eat paper covered with words, the ocean and its ships, the yellow dust of the sky and the red clay of the earth, yet nothing can cure their insatiable, ferocious hunger.

Feroce

My lover, who has lived in Korea for ten years and still speaks Korean with a French accent, still sees nothing wrong with wearing his hair long, still does not feel the need to be a company man with a steady salary or government bureaucrat with an iron rice bowl. My lover, after ten years living in the country of his birth near his Korean mother, is still treated as a foreigner in everyday life, whenever we're in the market, when we go to the movies, any kind of daily transaction. My lover has become slightly famous in Korea with a name that is neither his birth name nor his adoptive name, a name that is nowhere legal but completely invented but real, because that is what he calls himself.

My friends say that if he cut his hair, he wouldn't be mistaken for a foreigner. If he stopped being an artist and became an office worker, he could have kept his last Korean girlfriend. If he stopped being so flamboyant, so Francophone, so himself, people wouldn't ask him what he is.

My friends tell me that if I dressed more like a Korean woman, I wouldn't be mistaken for a foreigner. In the countryside, if I wore my hair long, I wouldn't be mistaken for a man. Korean American men tell me that maybe they'd be more interested in me romantically if I acted more Korean. It's the way I use my hands, look straight at other people, make direct statements, and challenge older people and my superiors if I disagree—my behavior is so *not* Korean. It doesn't matter what assets of personality I have built up in the U.S.—only what I lack. Korean American men often want to date Korean women so they can improve their Korean language skills—no help here. Even though I sometimes say I am a Korean American just because everyone in Korea knows what a *jaemi gyopo* is, but they don't necessarily know what an overseas adoptee is, I know that a basic difference between me and a jaemi gyopo is that Korean Americans have probably at least seen one adult Korean relative around while growing up, and I think that must mean something. I've observed enough Korean women to be able to mimic their behavior if I want to. But here I run up against the same problem as I did as a classical pianist, that of removing myself by just one step, so as to become only a conduit for the music: an interpreter, but not a composer. The best interpreters can insert themselves into someone else's music, and explore it so fully, finding every possibility, that in the end, they can make a piece almost entirely their own. But I was never a good interpreter, never a comfortable performer. I could never forget *myself* long enough to convincingly perform someone else's music, someone else's words, someone else's behavior, someone else . . .

Medical Korea: famous for dubiously cloning a dog and several other animals, and advancing plastic surgery technology to the point where ordinary-looking Korean women with enough money can purchase faces that look vaguely "Western" and therefore more beautiful. In a country where people believe your fortune and personality are spelled out on your face, it's not a waste of money to invest in a little surgery to make things right. You can get almost anything fixed to possess beauty here—bigger eyes, slimmer noses, narrower jawlines, skinnier calves, super-sized breasts. Even children can have surgery; why not get the eyelids done as a high school graduation present? Or, if you want something done as early as elementary school, why not have the connective tissue of the tongue cut in order to speak English better? No job is too big or too small for medical Korea! Unless, of course, the surgery has to do with children's problems that Americans think Koreans just do not have the technology for, such as harelips or clubfeet. Those children possessing the double whammies of congenital medical problems plus poor families have to get adopted before they can get medical treatment.

South Korea hopes to build its medical tourism industry, and it has the right materials to do that one day: compared to the cost of health care in the U.S., Korean medical treatment is cheap, and all Korean doctors speak some English, since they use Western medical terms. So although the medical infrastructure is not yet strong enough to support non-Korean-speaking tourists, I know that I can always get what I need if I can just talk with the doctor.

But first, I have to talk with the receptionist. On this afternoon, I am hoping that we will play the game of Give the Foreigner What She Wants and Then She Will Go Away. Instead, it appears that we are going to play Tell the Foreigner to Sit Down but Don't Call the Doctor so She'll Get Tired of Waiting—and Then She Will Go Away. But I don't have enough energy to go somewhere else and play the whole game again. I remain seated.

Right now I just want medicine for a sinus infection, but as in any Korean hospital, the mundane mixes with the dramatic. Several people with broken arms are walking around the waiting room, as are people in wheelchairs with broken legs, a few in hospital pajamas with IVs attached, and one man with a heavily bandaged hand, who appears to have gotten in some kind of terrible accident with a machine probably less than an hour ago. He has come to the right place. I think this hospital specializes in sewing people back together; the pictures on the walls of the hospital waiting room are of Before and After.

Before Example 1: Severed fingers laid next to the hand, greenish white on the outside and red on the inside.

After Example 1: The fingers stitched back on to the hand and miraculously pink.

Before Example 2: A photograph of the side of a man's torso and arm, skin peeled back and the arm completely mangled. Looks like an industrial accident. Looks like beef roast.

After Example 2: Everything is almost fine again, though a little puffy, but all the arm parts have been sewn back in there like you'd sew the stuffing back into a rag doll.

Before! After!

The adoptees told Bad Dominique that if he had just gotten the correct foreigner visa before the deadline, Immigration wouldn't have thrown him into the foreigner jail for a month. He thinks that he's not a foreigner so why should he need a foreigner visa. I don't know whose logic is broken, his or everybody else's. The French government would have come to his rescue if he had promised to go back to France in plastic handcuffs and not return to Korea for two years, but he wouldn't make that promise. He said jail was crowded and the Chinese couldn't understand why he was in there. A kind woman brought him a bilingual Bible in Korean and English, so he used it as a pillow—he couldn't read it anyway. The adoptees have been telling him this whole time that he should learn Korean, but he writes his diary longhand in notebooks, in French, and stores them in boxes at friends' houses. He says his language is his identity. The adoptees, eager to help each other in the "community" and all experts of their own "adaptation" to "Korean society," tell him that he should really get an apartment or at least a boardinghouse, but he says he is homeless anyway. "You don't think about what you'll eat until you're hungry, and I don't think about where I'll sleep until I'm tired. There are so many hotels in Seoul," he says. "If it's warm I sleep outside." He sleeps in saunas, friends' rooms, bars. He doesn't mind wearing ill-fitting clothes or having chronic eczema on his eyelids and neck. In mid-December, I saw him with his notebook in McDonald's, and it was -10 degrees Celsius and he had lost his phone. He had lost his passport. He had also lost his scarf. The next week, I gave him my scarf, which he lost at a basement bar within two days. Later he got another phone, and then gave it away to another French adoptee. Then he gave his winter coat to another adoptee in exchange for a thin striped shirt. "It's cold but at least I can feel something strong," he said.

I am sure that if I were braver, I'd be like him. I wouldn't even try to pass. I would just live.

Even with full command of the language, no accent, and all the necessary cultural accoutrements, including a white family, I still could not pass in rural Minnesota. So why do I think I could pass here? No matter how good my Korean gets, there is the problem of my accent, and those anxiety-producing instruments of dread commonly referred to as "telephones." *"What? What? We don't rent to foreigners."* There is the problem of Jae-dal's face. The problems of his face are the same and different as Joon-seung, whose mother married an African American military man. When Joon-seung tells people (in Korean) that he is Korean, they flatly say, "No you're not." That is slightly different than when people ask Jae-dal (in Korean) if he's sure his mother is Korean. That is slightly different than when I have a whole conversation (in Korean) with a merchant, and then he asks me, "Why don't you speak Korean?" We teach English to pay the rent.

English idiom: "The best of both worlds."

Yet we are still here. Every day for one year, three years, five years, ten years, thirteen years, we endure. In Korean, there are two kinds of "endure," one for enduring a short time and one for enduring a long time. Our situation calls for the long one: 견디다: *kyeondida*: to endure; bear; stand; put up with; tolerate.

In small shops in Seoul, it's not uncommon for me not to be able to complete a transaction before I explain the riddle of my face and tongue. Usually I satisfy their curiosity, but on Bad Korea Days I have walked out of shops leaving all my goods at the cash register because

I just don't feel like justifying my existence for someone else's entertainment or categorization (Korean born and raised in Korea, Korean born and partially raised in Korea but lived overseas for a long time and then returned, Korean born somewhere else but raised in Korea, American ethnic Korean, Japanese ethnic Korean, ethnic Korean from somewhere else, generation one, one-and-a-half, two, or more, Chinese, Japanese, Mongolian, student, student at Sogang, student at Yonsei, adoptee, overseas adoptee, domestic adoptee, reunited with mother, not reunited with mother, do have a boyfriend, don't have a boyfriend, do like Korean men, don't like Korean men). For this reason, I am a dedicated shopper at Grandmart in Sinchon, where there is little interaction with clerks and all the items are bar-coded at the same wonderful egalitarian price for all. A pot at Grandmart costs four thousand won for everyone. But at Namdaemun Market, supposedly the cheapest market in town, the same pot costs twice as much for foreigners:

"How much is this pot?"

"Are you Japanese?"

"No, I'm Korean."

"Is that so? Eight thousand won."

Another logic puzzle: why is it that Korean shopkeepers will insult Japanese people in Korean, assuming I am Japanese and assuming I don't understand, and then five minutes later speak to me (in Korean) and expect me to understand and have a conversation with them?

Although I discovered on a weekend trip to China that in Beijing, I am instantly recognizable on the street as Korean, in Korea I know better than to claim I am Korean. No matter how much I try to erase it, I still speak Korean with a rural Minnesota accent. I have learned to say these phrases:

"I am an overseas adoptee."

"I came and went from the U.S."

"I am your countryman!"

I have also learned these phrases:

"Shit, that's annoying."

"Why do you do that? Stop it."

"What does it matter to you?"

"Don't you have any manners?"

I have not yet learned how to say, "This is what a Korean person looks like and sounds like. Haven't you ever met a Korean before?"

My efforts to learn the Korean language begin to look more and more like a prolonged exercise in futility and lost wagers. Any grammar having to do with the Korean perception of time—forget it. My language teacher had claimed that Koreans are always late in the past tense, even if they're calling to say they're late an hour in advance, because at the time they call they're already late. Appointments made for the future but already agreed upon also exist in the past tense, even though they haven't happened yet. And while every Korean student of English seems to know there are twelve English verb tenses, I haven't yet met a Korean who knows how many Korean verb tenses there are. However, my teacher had said that there are only three native tenses—past, present, and future—and everything else has been made up to mimic English. I suppose that's why it's correct in Korean to say, "What do?" instead of "What are you doing?" Another problem is the intuitive, high-context nature of Korean, which means that leaving out the subject of a sentence is perfectly fine, which in turn means that I might understand perfectly well that someone is supposed to do a certain activity, but I have no idea who is supposed to do it. Other problems are simply vocabulary. Why is it that almost every adoptee I know took a month just to learn the word *kajok*? In Korean, "family" can be an easy word to parrot, but hard to remember. Meanwhile Chinese and Japanese students, studying for a university requirement or in the hopes that they can get a job in Korea one day, surpass us easily in class.

My elder Korean brother, my aunts and uncles, and my elder sister are disappointed that I'm not learning more quickly. I try to tell my sister that I'm losing my motivation to study because of my everyday interactions with Korean people—all the questions, the constant chore of explaining why I exist. I feel like a unicorn: a fantasy creature—the subject of movies, TV shows, pop songs, and books, but mythic and therefore imaginary, i.e., *not real*. Imagine if you should meet a unicorn! Oh, the questions you'd ask! Of course my sister, who has spent her life in Korea, understands Korean people—not American people like me. She tries to understand my discomfort intellectually, and explains the difference between Western privacy and Korean privacy (or lack thereof) to me, adding that these questions are how Korean people show love. I learn the words for "cultural difference," "failure," and "hurt feelings."

Those are the days when living in Korea feels like those mornings when, even before you step outside the door, you can feel that the weather conditions and barometric pressure are just exactly right to trap all the pollution of Seoul in between the mountains and the earth underneath a tight pressure lid, and it'll suffocate you all day and all night, make your sinuses swell and make you wish you were back in Minnesota lake country.

Still, there are days, many of them, when it's a wonderful just to spend another day in Korea. Happy just to live, no matter how marginally. Happy to ride the subway surrounded by Korean people even in the middle of cold and flu season. Happy to see mountains in the middle of a city. Happy just to eat Korean food, my favorites being kids' street cart fare: hodduk—a round, hot bread with molten brown sugar inside; boongeobbang—batter bread fried in the shape of carp fish with sweet red bean paste inside; and "toast"—two pieces of bread fried on a hot buttered griddle, with ham, eggs, a cheeselike square, cabbage, carrots, onions, and a sweet sauce spread on the inside, folded in half and served in a paper cup, or sometimes in a square of cardboard with a paper napkin. Pass on adult delicacies like cow guts, fish face, and pig feet.

Much later, after I had developed better Korean language survival skills—but more important, survival skills for dodging sexism and xenophobia—I would find Korea to be a very convenient place to live. "I'm too lazy to go back to the U.S.," I told my friends, citing all the conveniences that come from living in a place where there are more than forty-eight million people jammed into a space half the size of Minnesota. Over three years into my journey, at the end of my first year of having the highest-paying and most enjoyable job I've ever had, at the news agency, I had learned to dodge most of the annoyances and just enjoy the fact that in Seoul, one is never far from a convenience store, a coffee shop, a PC room with computers rented by the hour, a shoe repair shop, or a little Korean fast-food restaurant that serves nutritious food. I can usually hail a taxi within minutes if I don't feel like taking one of the world's most efficient public transportation systems. One is also never far from a post office, where the workers are friendly and helpful, and will let you use the tape, glue stick, and markers for free. One never has to make a reservation for lodging in Korea; cheap lodging is plentiful everywhere in the country. And since I'm Korean in body, the clothes always fit and the haircut is always right.

But despite my love of Seoul, I think I'm happiest in Korea at my brother's countryside house in the southernmost province, in his village populated almost entirely by members of his clan. The first grandfather of my brother's family can be traced back to the Koryeo dynasty in the Western year 960. My brother's most famous ancestor became famous by deciding that the truth was more important than life, so he told the king the truth, and he was executed. My brother's family's land includes fields and a mountain that is the family burial ground, and at the gate to the path leading up that mountain, all the generational names of his family are carved into a granite tablet. My brother is the first son of the twenty-third generation, keeper of all the Confucian rituals that hold his clan together.

I had just learned the Korean word for "half" and used my new vocabulary to ask my brother if he is technically my family, because I have a different father than he does. He said matter-of-factly, "We have the same mother." I kept insisting and asked whether the correct word for him is half brother or something else, but there is no such thing as "half brother" in Korean, according to him. He is just my brother.

My brother treats me as his family because he loves me and because he can. Unlike my sisters, he is not someone's daughter-in-law, a foreigner within her own family. He invites me to come to his house for *Chuseok,* the Korean harvest holiday. For Chuseok, amid the mounded graves of my brother's ancestors, my nephew and I gather chestnuts from trees and tear open the green prickly outer layers with our shoes. On my brother's lands the sesame and sweet potatoes, apples and pears, pumpkins and *jae pi* berries grow profuse and rich. A long time ago, these were the same fields and mountains that my mother worked as a daughter-in-law. A long time ago, my mother lived in the same house where my brother still lives, which is the house where she gave birth to him, and the same house where my brother's father died while my brother was still in my mother's womb. It was the same house where my brother's uncles grew up, and where my own mother helped to raise them. Even though I knew her less than a year—most of that year being a time, as an infant, that I cannot remember—I continue to live with my mother's traces all around me.

How to get there: Take Line 2 and get off at Sinchon subway station. Come out of exit 3 or 4 and walk behind the McDonald's. Turn right by the tie shop and you'll see a man selling hats. Walk up the hill and turn left at GS 25 convenience store. Pass several love motels, then turn left again at the big church. Look for the *Mirae* i-biz OneRoomtel sign at the top of a white building. Mirae means "future."

Here we are, all of us adoptees ostensibly studying the Korean language at local universities, and voluntarily living in the same institution-style "oneroom" buildings! Onerooms and their close cousins, boardinghouses, are not orphanages, so there's no more sleeping together on the floor—unless we really want to—since we all have our private rooms and beds down the hall behind numbered doors. But still it's twenty pairs of shoes parked in the shared entryway. We have a shared bath and kitchen—communal rice, soup, and kimchi—and no idea when someone will just up and leave the country. *No kidding, we're really from the same orphanage?! But they sent you to Denmark? We might have shared a crib! We should make T-shirts for all the graduates. You're class of '71? That makes you my* seonbae. *I'm class of '72. I'm your* hubae. *So buy me a snack. Someone call Korea Social Service. I want letter jackets.*

They sent you *where?*

For how long time have you been here?

How many are there in Italy?

Why are there so many adoptees from Minnesota?

Minnesota girls are kind of twisted.

I know you like the Eurotrash.

Well, you like Americans.

It's OK with Americans one-on-one, but when there's a whole bunch of them together . . .

Are you 'angry?

No, of course not. Why?

I didn't eat dinner. I'm 'angry.

I'm hungry too. Let's eat.

I am tired to speak English with you.

I came speaking only Norwegian. I learned English in Korea.

I can't understand the Dutch at all. Only your roommate.

I can't understand English. I can only understand you.

I don't go with adopteds.

Just your adopted friends.

Right.

Are you boring?

No, I'm having fun.

Sometimes I 'ate myself.

What?

I 'ate myself.

Oh, you hate yourself.

I love my language.

I am proud of my dialect. Even in Copenhagen I speak my dialect.

He sounds like a country boy.

No, only Americans have cheese Danishes.

What is the meaning of French vanilla?

Scandinavians and Americans are too worried about bacteria.

You are so sensible.

You mean I'm sensitive.

Are you hungry again?

Yes, I'm 'angry. Do you want to eat glass?

More than you know.

OK, let's go to Baskin-Robbins.

Norwegians don't say "I love you."

So that's what's wrong with Minnesota. It's Norway's fault. Tell your mother.

Sexual misery is a real problem, no?

Pyuntae-ya. Pervert.

Do you say "I love you" in English?

Pabo-ya. Stupid.

Excuse me.

You're welcome.

Je t'aime.

I love you.

Saranghae.

Strangers—

The property of what you can become obsessed by when you see an "available child" in a catalogue—

That which makes this one your adoptive mother—

The property of what matches in two people, like the pain in an absent limb—

That which makes this one your lover—

The property of whom you can become obsessed by, when you see her in an open window—

That which makes this one your stalker—

The property of who finds you alone on a certain day—

The property of what passes as love—

When a beautiful fairy tale crumbles in your hands, what remains?

In a life half a world away, you remember the steps you correctly followed like the choreography of an elaborate mask dance. You did everything you were supposed to, the leitmotif of *enough* ruling your life: enough food, enough loyalty, enough love. Good enough, lovable enough, malleable enough, you intuited the wishes of the people you cared about, the people whose respect you wanted, all of those family, friends, and strangers, was it ever really enough—

My lover says he wants to be nameless in this book of my life. I say what's new about that. What is new about your erasable Korean mother, or your mother's shame when you tell a restaurant owner that you are her son? What is new about the disaster combination of our faces and our speech, our inability to be identified by Koreans as anything, their way of arguing with us whether or not the Korean vocabulary that we use to describe ourselves and our families even exists: *saengmo,* birth mother; *haewei ibyangin,* overseas adopted person, not overseas adopted child. What is new about the picture our names create in other people's minds—who they think we are, who we really are, and the spaces in between? What is new about being homeless, almost without nationality and with only thin traces of family remaining? What is new about our artificial histories, how as we near the middle of our lives, we have seven names, six birthdays, five mothers, and five fathers between the two of us. Nearly unrecognizable, we pull the batteries out of the clock, tear down the calendar, disregard measurements of time, and decide, for once, upon a time that is purely our own.

If we are fools, reckless with our hearts, somehow disabled by our adoptions, made crazy from our time in orphanages and all the lapses in time between orphanages or in transit when we seem to have not existed; if we have been damaged from violence and the act of our bodies and lives being handed over, for a price, to complete strangers, why wouldn't we try to salvage what remains of our precious humanity? If you know this is all you have left in your heart, with what courage you can muster up despite all the disappointment you've already held, despite your doubt that you even have the ability to truly love another person, despite your doubt in your own judgment, why wouldn't you gamble each and every scrap of what remains on one chance to be happy? Wouldn't you take just one more chance on your own humanity, even if that chance came to you in a strange and sudden way?

So when your lover asks you to live with him after knowing you less than a week, you agree. You carry your cardboard boxes and suitcase to his house and make a new home. You wonder when was the moment that the man who was your lover became someone else—not a lover, not a husband, not really a boyfriend—but something wholly other, with no contract, no vows of permanency or everlasting love, but only the present and a wish to be, for once, happy.

Pabmeogeosseo? Have you eaten? is a standard greeting in a wealthy country fixated by its own starvation during the old days of poverty. After so many greetings, you realize that you too have been starving, and that is why you allow the logic of your hunger to guide you. Who knew that a Korean man's body looks like this, like your own? Who knew that makes a difference? You ask him to stop wearing that French cologne, because you want to know his smell, and you ask him to come in your mouth, because you want to know his taste. You spend hours touching him, massaging him, caring for his body. You notice everything because everything is new, and everything stands for something bigger than itself. Beauty marks on his right jawbone creep up onto the back of his neck like a constellation. There is something about the curve of his upper lip. You find the place where his spine is crooked, all his scars, all his asymmetries; you learn to read his day from the state of his fingernails at night. This part of intimacy feels good, on the primitive and instinctual level of Korean body to Korean body, not white man to Korean woman, not white mother to Korean daughter. Our bodies are what we know for sure. But in sleep, his hair, even longer and blacker than your own, spills across the pillow like the parts of each other that we do not know, and you wonder what he dreams about and if the content of his dreams intersects with your own—your adoptive parents who abandoned you only in a different way, your lovers of the past, the places you never want to see again but miss anyway. Does he dream of all his childhood toys that he will never touch again, the comic books and the vinyl records? Does he dream of his paternal grandmother who brought him to the orphanage without his mother's knowing? Does he dream of how his Korean mother never forgot him, not even for one day? Does he dream of a return to somewhere? You wonder whether he dreams in French, Korean, or English.

Here you are, two nearly anonymous people living without rules, by authority purely your own, without need of convincing anyone. You have memorized the geometry of his body, and have laid it across the arc of your heart. How easy it is to simplify your life to this—cooking, eating, sleeping, washing. How natural it is for you to wake together, when the floor becomes too hot, and make love in the pale blue light of early morning, dawn, *saebyeok*.

You think it's possible that your mother loved your father once, and that you were conceived in this same way, somewhere in this beautiful terrible city, two Korean bodies entwined, rising and falling, tension and release.

발음: *pareum:* pronunciation
바람: *param:* a desire; wish; hope
바람: *param:* a motive; a consequence

바람: *param:* a wind; a breeze

바람 났어: *"Param nasseo."* "You're like the wind." (Idiomatic expression implying a changeable mind and/or whorishness. An appropriate situation in which to use this expression: when a plain woman who always stays in her room and studies and never dresses up suddenly "makes" a boyfriend, dresses up, and goes out all the time.)

After a while, you notice the residue. You can tell, on the street, what used to be cigarettes, what used to be spit, what was spilled. That smell is the stink of gingko nuts, and soon the yellow leaves will turn to dust underneath the pedestrians' feet. You identify the living residue of an ongoing occupation: English teachers and military men. English teachers wear a uniform of one kind, the military another, but both are recognizable without uniforms. Every day at 3:00 the same U.S. military man in civvies walks out of the intersection between Itaewon 1-dong and Itaewon 2-dong, emerges from the English-graffitied underpass at Boksakkot Street, and walks toward Noksapyeong station exit number 2, next to the U.S. base, where Korean police stand stiffly on guard at the subway stairwell. Sometimes it is the regular police and sometimes it is the riot police. Every day, the same barbed wire pricks its way across the sky, the same neon red cross of the Christian church's steeple makes the same kind of commentary behind the same uniformed men with rifles guarding the gate at the military base, where you turn right to walk home. When you go to the movies you take the shortcut behind Yongsan station, where the prostitutes apply makeup even while waiting on display in their neon red boxes, the same neon red as the butchers' windows in another part of the city, the same red as every cross. You wonder why, in lights, they only have this one shade of red: sex red, meat red, motel red, Konglish red, Jesus died for your sins red, Korea at night red.

In the district where you were born, you begin to understand your father's rage. First there was your sister, the one who was sent away with you, light-skinned for a Korean and assumed to be half-American in a public setting such as this, packed with a foreign military. And then you came along, also light, when your father was already "suspicious of his wife's chastity." You think of your father, who was also a man, walking past American soldiers carrying rifles who ate meat every day. Your father was an *ajeossi*.

Your mother was an *ajumma*. Ajummas live for hiking, picnics, children, and their ajumma friends. At the market, she always haggles for the best prices. She shoves you out of her way as she carries packages on her head wrapped in pink *pojagi* cloths. She can carry an entire tray of food for four people on her head. When she eats, her mouth no longer has a beautiful eating shape. She eats kimchi straight out of the jar and doesn't bother to cut it, tilting her head back instead and dropping it into her mouth with chopsticks. When she drinks soju, she can drink as much as a man, and she makes a guttural sound in the back of her throat after she takes a shot. Before the rest of the city wakes, she goes to markets and buys fruits and vegetables and then resells them on the street. She makes rice cakes, kimbap, and sandwiches at home, then sits in the cold all day chanting for someone to buy her food. She cooks food inside a tent all day and often all night, sleeping inside her *pojangmatcha* or behind her fruit stand.

You are still searching for your mother's face. So on the street it's not the rich ajumma with the perfect hair, makeup, manicure, and designer suit whom you see. You see only the fiercely proud ajumma sitting outside in the freezing cold selling dried beans and vegetables. And you are still searching for your father's face, compulsively turning the present around to gaze upon the past, a blank circle of wood, the face of your dead father, a face you never saw in life. So even though there are Korean men who are hardworking, caring, and gentle, like your brother or brothers-in-law, your eyes are instead drawn to the exception, the embodiment of the disoriented and struggling Korea that you were born into, the man who has failed his family, the man who has spent his money on his friends but not his wife, the man who is mentally ill, the man who is most like your father. This ajeossi is the e who goes home and says there's nothing to eat, so his ajumma wife looks in the cupboards and finds the ingredients for a soup to please him. This ajumma can absorb her husband's sexual energy before he passes out drunk and can make his unwanted babies with it. When her husband's lovers call late at night, she bears it. When he drinks with his coworkers in room salons, where young women are paid to "entertain" men, she bears it. When he doesn't come home at all, she bears it. A drunk ajeossi will vomit in the subway train cars or fall down the subway stairs and lie there on his face. He will sleep wherever he falls down. He will urinate and spit on the street. He will become jobless and ride the city buses aimlessly, wearing a suit and reeking of sweat and alcohol. When he loses his job, he will prostrate himself at subway entrances, bowing with forehead touching the ground, legs bent beneath him, palms upward. Sometimes he will not bow, but will sit with a cardboard box in front of him waiting for someone to drop some change in, after which he empties the box, deposits the change in his pocket, and begs for more. He might be injured or handicapped, but more often he appears perfectly able-bodied. Some beggars are neighborhood fixtures and some are transient, but nearly all are male. In my first two years in Korea, I saw only four female beggars: one blind, one legless, one old and crazy, one carrying a child.

As a general rule, Korean women do not beg.

Inquieto

You thought, the ostinato of your life is an aliveness close to destruction.

You thought, sometimes a melody floats above, but the harmony that binds life together is voiced in a texture always violent.

You thought, scattered about you is the residue of what you tried to make permanent: marriage, family, nationality, normality. Broken promises and failed good intentions are the debris of your life. When has anything been permanent? Why would it start now? So you stopped living in someone else's story, you stopped playing someone else's notes, you stopped contorting yourself trying to be someone you are not. You thought, rules are not for me. You gave up on authority and false attributions of it. You thought to burn through everything—the rulebooks, the expectations, the books of notes—and play this life by ear.

But at some point, time shifted in your mind. You slipped out of the present and into the future because you wanted it to work this time. You wanted permanency, and you became attached, you included him in your plans. He included you in his. You met his Korean mother, discussed what country to live in together, keeping Korea as a home base, and whether you'd like to live Korean-style with his mother or alone, in Seoul or in the countryside. Together you decided to name the house. It was his idea to name it "Permanency." You were so hungry that you bought it, ate it, believed it.

Yet again and again, the patterns of thought and action are laid out like train tracks throughout the subterrain of your life. You could blame the patterns on neurobiological damage from trauma or adoptee psychological problems, whether his or yours: preemptive strikes, threats to leave, inability to feel love, inability to give love, geographic escapes, psychic homelessness, craving intimacy, fearing intimacy, gorging on "love" but choking on each mouthful. To yourself, you try to explain your actions, your hunger, your loneliness and longing in the red red city of Seoul, the way it forces your adoptee freakishness to stand out in relief, the way you have to explain yourself, your existence, every day, in every shop, every taxi: "No, I'm not Japanese, I'm an adopted Korean," followed by the predictable reactions, your long-ago happenstance country of adoption so much more fascinating to Koreans than the country where you were born and where you fight to live now.

You realize that every day has made you into a liar because you are tired of explaining why you are the way you are, so sometimes you say you're Japanese, other days, Chinese, other days, Korean American, and you notice that he lies too, everyday interactions being easier and shorter because everyone knows why a Korean would end up in the U.S., but a small country in Europe would need more explaining. At the immigration office, when you're confronted with the blank lines asking for your "Duration of Visit" and "Purpose of Visiting Korea," don't think too hard about the future or make existential explanations. The easy way to do it—and you might be surprised at how you can construct your whole life to make things easier—is to lie. Just lie! Write "two years." Write "study." Your official documents that got you adopted are all lies anyway, so what's another lie on another government paper? Introducing yourself to strangers as a piano teacher with no piano is pretty weird, but every Korean knows what a student is and *haksaeng* is an easy word to remember. So one day you study at Sogang University, the next day you study at Yonsei, the next day, Ewha. It's important to lie when you tell your Korean family that you're fine. *Life is easy here, don't worry about me.* Lie when you go to parties and by all means try to act "normal"—if you can even remember what that looks like—so people think you're busy and productive instead of lonely or needy or sad because no one, not even an adoptee, wants to be the friend of a lonely needy sad person. You learn that the more you lie, the easier it gets. It's so easy to lie in a language not your own. You can lie all day in Korean and it doesn't even make you flinch, and the parts you don't want to hear or don't want to answer, just pretend you don't understand. You learn that the skill of lying transfers to English quite well. You learn that your lover has also developed his skills of lying, but despite his lies to you about your value to him because you are an adoptee who can understand him, you learn the truth—that he actually prefers Real Korean Women ("It's just something about them"), and despite your lies to everyone else about your identity, he knows that you are *not* a student, *not* Japanese, *not* Chinese, and most importantly, *not Korean.* You know that you cannot help him be more Korean or help him in this society, and without the help of a Real Korean Woman he will continue to sign contracts he can't read and will continue to fail in all his business endeavors, and the longer he looks at you the more ugly American you are to him—those gaping holes in femininity, those attitudes, those mannerisms, that awful accent. You try not to let your feelings get hurt because everybody, after all, has a right to their own preferences. You try not to feel like less of a woman. And you wonder if he prefers Real Korean Women because he also prefers a Real Language Barrier.

You remind yourself that you are trying to be better and more mature than you really are, and go back to thoughts of impermanency despite your wish for permanency, and of love as impermanent, indefinite, fugitive.

My lover, if I said to you that I could accept ambiguity and impermanency, what I didn't say is that I lied to myself and believed it, because I wanted to be better than I may be capable of ever being. Honestly I still wanted to make the rules about when you'd love me, for how long, and what kind of love you would give me. To that, all I can say is that at the center of my heart my only desire is to be loved intimately, for someone to love me as a whole person, for what I have unwillingly become. *What it is that I have become.* But I cannot dictate my wishes upon you, love itself, the people who made us, or this country that we live in that sometimes makes us into people we can no longer recognize.

In this country that pulses with the collective memory of an unfinished war, an artificial boundary etched through the middle of her body and the collective imprint of a desperation that will not go away, I am still at war with myself. How does one live in the condition of being separated from oneself? Separation turns into national obsession: war as theme park; adoptee as stock character who makes everyone cry when the sad music comes on; hokey movies about the destruction of family ties. National identity crisis turns into nationalistic fervor over an islet near Japan and parts of northeastern China that show traces of Korean culture; anti-Americanism is coupled with what seems like every student's desire to study in the U.S. There is the hysteria to learn

English, and the hysteria to date a foreigner in order to get even more, better, twenty-four-hour private tutoring. America, get the hell out but we would like to keep McDonald's and Starbucks. Japan, we still hate you, you imperialist sons of bitches, but we really like the Harajuku bags. Cultural trauma stemming from hemorrhoid-inducing starvation translates into the burning of Buddhist temples and fervent born-again Christianity. During Chuseok a nice gift to give is an expensive Spam gift package; look how nicely the joke food of Minnesota is incorporated into the haute cuisine of the occupied. If you don't have access to the U.S. military base and you still want Miracle Whip, you can buy your gray market goods in the alley in front of the room salon by Sinchon Grandmart, or in many other selected back alleyways near you. If you do have military friends, you can buy your American turkey or ham Thanksgiving dinner and have it delivered straight to your home, paper plates and everything. You can pay in dollars. Unfortunately you cannot buy clove cigarettes anywhere in Korea. That is a real shame because I think this country needs clove cigarettes. They taste like ham, but in Korea, I think they could sell a lot if they made them taste like Spam. No, I take that back—I don't know what it is that we really need here, cigarettes or otherwise, but we do have cheap alcohol and that is a fact. It is possible to get drunk for twenty-five cents courtesy of any convenience store and there are many. You can even ask for shot-sized paper cups. For fifty cents, you can get drunk with a date. You would drink too if you were at all Korean.

I fled the U.S. during its war against terror. The Americans had not yet taken the children of Afghanistan or Iraq for adoption, though they tried, because every war displaces family members and creates orphans. I had become more and more a foreigner in my own country, an unpatriot. I watched the effects of the fear of outsiders and the fear of ideas ripple throughout my neighborhood, the schools, the newspapers, the libraries, my friends, and their children. I watched patterns of occupation and violence unfold in the relentless way that patterns do, one after the other after the other. All I wanted was a safe place where I could have my thoughts and share them with someone I loved. And then there was Korea, in the way that I found her.

So inside my lover's house I created a safe place. It was my refuge from a hostile world.

Then he said, "You think too much."

And then, "I guess I don't know how to be with an American woman."

Then, "I don't feel like much of a man with you."

"You know I don't have work these days."

"For ten years I have lived as if every day would be my last. I spent all my money and cared nothing for the future."

"Did you forget we have only been together a few weeks? We are not a couple."

He said, "I don't want to have to care about you."

Thirty-six days passed. On the thirty-seventh day he asked me to leave. I would not beg. I spent that night by myself, and I dreamt of America. I dreamt I was in a hospital and we were all born or made damaged in some way and it was Christmas. I dreamt of elevators and stairs, of empty coat hangers, of my American parents who cared for me once, and then I dreamt of leaving: my first dream of Korea. I dreamt of the big cement bridge with its colorful mural at the edge of Itaewon, and the taxi I would ride away from my home. My sadness did not leave me. Nights after that, I dreamt of fire. All night, fires set intentionally and unintentionally billowed inside my mind, consuming people and houses. Holy men burned themselves silently on prayer rugs while I sat next to them. I watched their faces. I woke nearly asphyxiated. Then there were the other dreams, waiting for guests who did not come, inside a big house with a foyer that looked out onto a garden. Inside the house there was an unused room for children, an old and unused piano, an ancient rocking horse. I knew the immensity of the room from its acoustics, the sound of the heels of my shoes tapping against the marble floor of a large room with no furniture, and the way my ankles and waist were slim, my womb empty.

I had imagined a wooden sign with the name of our house hung over our door. But we had only succeeded in hanging a paper sign: 주차금지. *Jucha geumji.* No Parking. I took the bus to the subway and found a new place to live. It was Monday. One room. One window. One desk. One narrow bed. I watched the sunlight change as it lit the window frame from different angles. All day I watched the sun move. In the days following I learned its pattern, how in the morning a bright rectangle appeared on my wall, and moved slowly all afternoon, changing shape. In the afternoons the sun lit the dust on the sill, the cream-colored curtains, and the oily red bricks of the exterior, their edges casting shadows upon their own repetition, one after the other, brick shadow mortar, brick shadow mortar, one after the other, every man I have shared a bed with, this accumulation of absence, these patterns of departure.

It occurred to me that I had spent my life going back and forth between two opposite points on the globe and had missed everything in between. I thought, I could try traveling alone. Lots of women do it. I could go anywhere from Korea: Beijing and Tokyo are only two hours away by airplane. Or I could take the ferry from Busan to the southern islands of Japan. I could send postcards from the ocean. I heard that in Shanghai, people are open to foreigners and different ways of doing things. I heard that in Kuala Lumpur and Singapore, people speak English and they don't ask you where you're from. I could go to Europe to learn biodynamic farming or just to be a tourist. I could apply for any number of writers' workshops; I've never been to Provincetown. I could go to school again and get a master's degree or even a Ph.D. I could even go back to Minneapolis and hang with my girlfriends on Lake Street and eat at Little Tijuana or our favorite Vietnamese noodle restaurant. I could live in temples and eat tofu and meditate. I could do anything, anywhere. I have no ties to make me feel guilty, no one else's needs or emotions to consider, no one to care about, nothing to hold me down.

Without a lover, I have such exquisite, cruel freedom.

Chapter Six

Dolente

With about twenty-one tons of tension holding together the metal frame, wood, and wire of a grand piano, every instrument is bound to have a weak spot. On my piano, the weak spot was the E a tenth above middle C. It was always the first note to go out of tune—out of tune with itself, the three strings fighting each other, and out of tune with the other Es and the rest of the piano. The way this piece sounded on my piano always reminded me of weeping, the hammer striking again and again at the weakest part of my instrument.

외: 外: *wei:* outer; foreign
외가: 外家: *wei ga:* the home of one's mother's parents
외손: 外孫: *wei son:* one's daughter's child
외족: 外族: *wei jok:* maternal relative
외탁하다: 外- *wei takhada:* to take after one's mother's side
of the family
외도하다: 外道: *wei do hada:* to stray from the right path
외국인: 外國人: *wei guk in:* a foreigner; an alien
외국어: 外國語: *wei guk eo:* a foreign language
외구: 外寇: *wei gu:* a foreign enemy; a foreign invader
해외입양: 海外入養: *hae wei ibyang:* sea outside enter nourish,
i.e., overseas adoptee
외계: 外界: *wei gyeo:* the external world
외각: 外殼: *wei gag:* a shell; a crust

It is publicly argued how much I write is true and whether the truth matters, what kind of truth is mine, who is entitled to my mind and body, what I can possibly know of anything after a rupture of this magnitude—

Here is what I know of the truth:

Bill Thornton is now a butcher. Chad Patton is a policeman. But thirty years ago they were my kindergarten classmates, and they had me pinned underneath the farthest tree from the school building, where no one could hear me screaming, because I didn't want their bodies on top of mine, and I didn't want their kisses.

I wonder what happened to Mr. Becker, the elementary school gym teacher. I wonder if he's still teaching wrestling, and if he's still taking little girls out of class for special testing in the boiler room.

Clyde Burgess, he's dead. When I heard the news I was relieved, not so much for myself as for the other little girls who might have to sit on his lap in his wheelchair every week for the school's foster grandparent program, and feel his old man's hands.

My adoptive grandpa, Evan Walsh, is also dead. At his funeral, my mom and aunts criticized him for his treatment of their mother, although they never criticized their mother for not protecting them from him. There must have been a reason, though, why my mother fled to her own grandmother's house even before she graduated from high school.

Shawn Johnson, my best friend from high school, called me up out of the blue about a year ago. He said, I always loved you, but I didn't tell you. Remember that time when we were walking in the woods? I wanted to kiss you, but—do you remember our neighbor Lloyd? My mom had him babysit me for about ten years—and I couldn't touch you, because I didn't want to hurt you in that same way.

My stalker has been incarcerated since 1991. That's eighteen years now, and still counting. That's also good, because I am afraid of him, and I don't want him to come after me again. It's not the raping, killing, and videotaping part of his plan that bothers me the most, but the part where the police found a copy of a book called *Pearl Harbor* in his car.

If I had been born the first son of my Korean father—not his fifth daughter—I don't think he would have tried to smother me with a blanket when I was born. I probably would have grown up in Korea and continued my father's family line.

Bill Thornton and Chad Patton, I remember the outline of the branches of the tree against the afternoon sky, how the trunk looked with my head next to it, the feel of dirt on my face. Mr. Becker, I remember the blinding brightness of the lights on the ceiling, the gray steel door, closed, the roar of a furnace warming an entire Minnesota school in winter. What were you doing with me, alone in the boiler room, that I can't fully remember? In adulthood, a friend of my sister's said that he remembered me as the girl who threw up every day on the school bus because she didn't want to go to school. My mother gave me mint every morning to soothe my stomach before sending me out to the bus, but never asked what hurt my stomach. Clyde Burgess, my foster grandfather, I remember the chocolate from my mouth smeared on your shirt, how I struggled to get away, how I begged not to go but my parents made me see you—it was part of a school program—and I was made to give presents to you. Grandpa, I remember my mother and aunt standing at the sink, wondering what to do after you touched my sister, and then deciding to do nothing. Shawn, I remember how it felt when I wanted you to love me.

Who will defend a child whom no one believes, not even her own parents? Who will defend a child against her own parents? Childhood is risky anywhere. The risk is compounded by being born female in Korea. The risk is compounded again by being an Asian female in America.

Fight or flight: too small to fight with my fists, I have always had to choose flight. I fled the U.S., unable to bear the sight of yet another adopted child with white parents. Parking lot encounters, restaurant bathroom encounters, children's section in the library encounters drove me back to the motherland. But why should I believe that a place we call the motherland can protect me or give me rest? Korea doesn't exist except in its own people, like my mother. This is the country where my father took off my mother's nose with his teeth. This is the country where my father was jailed for violence against his family. I could ride the subway to Hannam-dong right now, and stand in the alley where I was born, or in the place where the house once stood, where my own father tried to kill me. *Aboji,* maybe war made you like that. Maybe that's where you found the bayonet. But now you are dead and I am still living, even with my shattered tongue, my blinded eyes.

What does "Meet me by McDonald's" or "Turn left at Pizza Hut" really mean, except that to adoptees, what is Western is always easier to see—Baskin-Robbins, Krispy Kreme, the American military, the English language, the fetishists so much more visible and happy here because everyone wants to be loved, even if they have to use their white privilege to get it. Because everyone wants to be loved, what is easy to see in summer is the white adoptive parents vacationing at tourist attractions standing in line at the Burger King before they take children from their motherland.

A Korean woman once told me this: "Life is fighting. Go and fight, then take a rest, then go and fight more. Fight every day." Is fighting what being Korean means?

For one year I lived in Korea without carrying ID and without carrying a business card, trying to be no one so that I would not have to fight to prove who I am. But in Korea, everyone must carry a "name card." *They are a tool to make connection,* a Korean person told me. They are exchanged at every first meeting of people, every party. Not having something to give feels awkward, rude.

Underneath the neon lights of the Sinchon neighborhood, the streets are littered with the cards of call girls with names like Strawberry. The mafia men who look like ordinary deliverymen distribute the pictures of women posing in lingerie in front of motel entrances, bending the cards in half and arranging them in rows so they are easier to pick up. The Korean love motels have English names: Seven Motel, Alps Motel, Motel Good Time, Saipan Motel, Motel Piano. Swiss Motel has nothing to do with Switzerland, the lit and spinning twin barbershop poles outside it have nothing to do with haircuts, and the Christmas decorations left up all year round do not mean Christmas. The love motels that do not mean love offer license plate covers to shield the identities of cars and drivers. They creep up the hills of a neighborhood that tastes of bus fumes and open sewers, and the loneliness and hope of university students, beggars, prostitutes, adoptees, and ordinary people.

In these damp and darkened streets the adopted men are fighting. They are fighting white men, Korean men, themselves. Somehow they need to hit and be hit and the hurting feels good.

—Hit me, hit me again. Finally someone understands me.

—If you hit me back I'll kill you.

—Hit me again, brother.

Inside windowless basement rooms in Seoul, adopted women cut marks into their arms, stay up all night calling places in the world where it is still daytime. Inside *noraebangs* and *sulchips* we are making slow violence upon our bodies with pitchers of pale Korean beer and green bottles of soju and and cheap lite cigarettes; inside motel rooms and DVD rooms rented by the hour, we are fucking whoever can make us feel loved for a few hours or one night, take your pick of how long you want to try, take your pick of how long you want to believe the promises of someone who lives only in the present, not even day by day or hour by hour, but minute by minute, crashing through the fulfillment of one desire, one compulsion, to the next.

Bad Dominique had the particular distinction of having lived in Sinchon as a baby, with his parents, and then again as an adoptee thirty years later. Over time I watched his beautiful brown skin, his clear and black eyes, change into the face of a man who cannot go without drink for even one day, the puffy red mask and the stink, the unkempt hair and torn clothing. I became more familiar with the Korean police than I had ever been with the American police. When his scalp was split open and blood was gushing out because a Korean had hit him over the head at Burger King, I realized that he would just accumulate another one of the same kind of marks on his scalp that he already had—marks that his birth mother had immediately looked for, without explanation, when they met again after all those years. His whole life has been the same fight, the same hurt.

I step carefully around the vomit and trash, disregard the injured stray cats, hope I will not find cockroaches inside my room. Once inside, I lock my door and write for hours. The words accumulate across the page like rows of soldiers. Bill, Chad, Clyde, my stalker, Mr. Becker, Grandpa, Mom, Dad, Aboji—what I am naming is not you, but the thing that is so large that it cannot fit into a boxing ring, the thing that I will take down with my own occupied mind, in the language of those who bought me, in this country that values only my monstrosity.

If we want to stop fighting, we should be able to. If we want to stop running, we should be able to. If we want to love, if we want to live, if we want to stop being lonely, if we have come this far just to be with each other, then we should be able to. Shawn, Jae-dal, Bad Dominique, the man I loved without a name, Carol, Umma—what I am naming now is you. I am naming why I want to live. I am naming the reason why this time, I will stay, and I will fight.

Chapter Seven

—◦—

Poetico

Desperation is close to nihilism and can look like global adventure. I was ten years old when I first felt the insatiable desire to move to a land far, far away. I counted the days of each remaining school year, and then of each remaining grade, until I could finally leave my hometown. I left when I was eighteen years old with all my possessions in the back of my dad's pickup truck, and in between then and now I have lost count of all the places I have lived, all the small rented rooms in other people's houses, all the one-bedroom garden-level apartments where the damp basement sewer smell is always the same. I know now that owning a two-story gingerbread-colored house with white frosting trim and scallops, filled with all the furniture that a middle-class husband needs to buy, suffocates me with the artificial requirement of happiness: *What else could I want? Why am I still not happy?* I feel better when I have few connections, few obligations, few things, no furniture. What was I thinking when I ripped up all the sod in the back lawn and planted a garden of vegetables, herbs, and flowers? The following summer I gave my friends all the perennials—the hollyhocks, coneflowers, rosemary, and strawberry vines. I had even told myself that I would wait a decade for the asparagus to mature, but that too I dug up by its roots and distributed in cardboard boxes with the rest.

I have moved so often that I have my own techniques for packing and carrying; I can pack up everything I own in less than two hours and go anywhere, live anywhere. I say to myself that if I have few things, I have fewer memories and in some ways this is good. They say that it's your personal things that make a place feel like home; I buy things that I don't really like so it's easier to throw them away later. I tell myself that when my exterior homelessness reflects my interior homelessness, I feel better.

My American mother is a champion pack rat, stockpiler of canned goods bought at wholesale prices, saver of scraps of fabric and spools of thread, shoebox filer of every Christmas, birthday, and anniversary card she ever got from anyone, keeper of her grandmother's housewares, hoarder of other people's things that she buys at rummage sales and auctions—Depression glass covered candy dishes, pitchers, tea sets, antique irons, place settings and tumblers for every holiday, and armoires, dining room sets, and rocking chairs all bought with the intent to refinish or reupholster someday but until then just stored in the basement, piled up to the ceiling with *things,* and with just three paths cleared for walking through the room: one to the deep freezer, another to the other deep freezer, and one to the refrigerator. Mom was terribly ashamed of her piles and never let guests go downstairs, but her shame didn't do anything to change how things were faring in the subterrain.

Whether despite or because of all those objects, the place that felt like home to me the longest was indeed my American parents' house. Upstairs: a three-bedroom one-and-a-half-bathroom rambler with tuck-under garage, perfect condition, lakeshore property. They have tended the garden, mown the lawn, painted neutral colors outside and applied fresh coats of eggshell white paint inside, and changed into the latest JC Penney–inspired styles at least once each decade. There are no squeaks in the floor. There is no mold, no dust, no scuff marks. The kitchen cabinets, original to the house, harbor no splatters of dirt or grease. Run your hand over them; they are perfectly smooth. Go ahead and look behind the refrigerator; I guarantee it is clean even back there. This perfect house has survived my alleged atheism, my bad poetry, my reliable night terrors, my bad paintings, my unwillingness to smile for photographs during the first seven years of life, several of my trips to psychiatric units, and one halfhearted suicide attempt in the tuck-under garage, in a '76 Chevy that failed to keep running. Yet all the decor matches. The stovetop sparkles. The windows are spotless. Their house is an example of how good things can be. This is the heartland of Americana.

My sister told me the news about Mom and Dad's upcoming move. They're moving to a one-level house to get them and their knees through old age, so they're building a house on a different part of their property. Their old house is now up for sale. It is has been on the market for over six months. Not one offer.

Mom had hesitantly told my sister that strange things have been happening over the past few years. Doors that Mom and Dad conscientiously locked when they left the house are unlocked when they come home. Dad finds his clothes in a heap, underneath the covers of the bed that Mom just made. They hear footsteps on the stairs at night.

"Alzheimer's?" I suggested to my sister.

"No," she says. "They're not crazy. Mom and Dad both see and hear these things. And you know how they are about locking the doors."

"How often does this happen?"

"I'm not sure, but Mom could tell you. She keeps track in a notebook."

Mom is hypergraphic in her own way. She keeps lists of events: births, deaths, anniversaries. She keeps a list of long-distance calls she made so she can check it against her phone bill later, a list of tasks to be completed. On Halloween, she knows exactly how many trick-or-treaters have visited. On the Fourth of July, a big holiday in lake country, she knows exactly how many cars have driven past our house. *Write it down,* I can still hear her saying, her answer to almost everything. Sometimes the lists backfired: her list of presents that she bought left out on the kitchen countertop ruined the surprises of at least one Christmas. But sometimes her list making was essential: when I was stalked she kept a list of encounters with my stalker and this turned out to be really important for the sheriff. Now she keeps a list of encounters with poltergeists.

I asked how long the poltergeists have been coming. My sister told me the date, and I noted to myself that the poltergeists started roughly when our family finally fell apart. The falling apart started a long time ago, but I think we finished falling when my Korean mother died, when I was twenty-eight years old, which was the same age my mother was when I fulfilled her desire to have a baby. My sister, who never had any illusions about who she was in our family, knew that what our mom desperately wanted was a *baby*—not a child almost old enough to go to school. My sister was four and a half when we were delivered to our American parents, and she was the free part of the buy-one-get-one-free deal, as she calls it.

Desperation is close to nihilism and can easily look like crime. Looks like an American Indian man in a mental asylum for stalking a Korean woman, looks like an adoptee in jail for the crime of claiming he is Korean, looks like the adoptee you'll never meet because he's in prison for stealing cars, looks like adoptees in juvenile detention centers and psychiatric units making stupid crafts out of wood, and the grim jokes we make about that useless therapy afterward: *can you believe they gave me that many drugs and then let me use a band saw?* Looks like men who've been dominated by the entire world for their entire lives so therefore won't take any domination at home, not even *Would you please come home to me,* looks like women bearing not only their own pain but also the pain of all their men.

—◦—

One of our professors at Inje University said that Korea is the "Land of Politeness." I think what he really meant to say is that Koreans have grammar and vocabulary rules for how to speak to older people and strangers. But strictly in terms of Western concepts of politeness, Koreans are, well, straightforward people. That means they say it right to your face.

—*Wah! Yeppeunaeyo!* Wow! You're pretty!

—You are really skinny. You look better in your picture.

—*Pabo-ya!* You're stupid!

—Where are you from? America? But you look like Korean. Where are you really from?

—Why did you come to Korea? Because YOU'RE KOREAN? Ha ha ha!!

—You're like a baby, you don't know anything!

—All men are bad . . . Kyong-ah, you have to get married, you know.

—Eat a lot! Don't drink so much water!

—Korean men are selfish . . . Marry a Korean man!

—Don't you like Korean men? I need a daughter-in-law. I know someone for you. Give me your phone number.

—Kyong-ah, your face is getting skinny.

—Kyong-ah, your face is getting fat.

—You have too many freckles. Hurry up and go to the skin clinic for that.

—Kyong-ah, you're getting old. You better hurry up and have a baby.

—Kyong-ah, go back to America and get married.

My adoptive mother has never been pregnant but has been a mother. My double daughterhood became absent motherhood, canceled out.

A farm girl married at eighteen, Mom took the Pill until she wanted children and then realized all the money she had wasted. Dad, sterile, was her first and only lover. Most of my friends back in Minnesota are married now and have kids, have stopped counting lovers, but here in Seoul we accumulate the knowledge of adults who love reflections of themselves indiscriminately.

Pills are cheap and condoms are free, my jutting hip blades took three adopted men within two years, enough for my Korean sister to tell me I am like the wind. I took them inside me as if I could internalize love but from out these blades I wonder what could ever come. *No, I have never been pregnant,* I had told the American doctor. *Yes, I am married but have never been pregnant not even once, no miscarriages, no abortions. No,* I said, *I have never been pregnant,* and the doctor had recommended genetic counseling for me and the husband of my childless marriage. Three years divorced and thirty-six years old, what could come from me—a child not Korean, not adopted, not European, not

American, not anything. My waist the width of a man's hand will never look like the soft white bread-dough figure of my adoptive mother, that maternal figure, good mother, breasts, hips, hair, German odor, *What's not to love?* you might ask, trays of sugar cookies and cinnamon rolls in the morning, hot roast beef sandwiches and green beans canned at home. *She gave you a better life.*

But I can never make up for what I never got. The arms and promises of a lover will never become a mother's nourishing breasts or the promises that she couldn't keep. With the departure of each consecutive lover in Korea, the person whom I pine for is my mother. Each night I think of her hand in mine and my imagination runs wild, wild, with the conversations I want to have with her, the arguments I want to have with her, the things I want to do with her—vacations on islands scattered around Korea, afternoons spent watching animal shows on TV or making acorn jelly, makkoli, kimchi, this physical love of the mother.

Even if my mother were here now, could she undo what has been re-created? In the long years of my adoption I had forgotten that Korean women too can give physical sustenance, that white women alone do not provide this. The sight of a middle-aged white woman on a Seoul street—a stranger, who, to my perpetual surprise, never recognizes my own whiteness—brings up memories of hamburger hotdishes with kidney beans, white bread and grape jelly, homemade beet and bean pickles; I am homesick for the kind of physical sustenance I associate with white people. At the two-year mark, my tongue, confused, grew tired of red chili peppers, garlic, salt, soy, and sesame every day, and rejected Korean food. My hard-won acquired taste for seafood, tofu, kimchi, and soju I let go as I couldn't stand the thought of one more piece of the national dish, one more drop of the national alcohol. The last things immigrants lose, they say, are their food and their language. My mouth, stuffed with English, had little room for the Korean language. Although my ears began to understand Korean, my tongue would always betray me with the unmistakable diphthongs of a native English speaker, a pianist who could never manage to play by ear. It took eleven years, not just one summer, to finally be able to enjoy the sounds of traditional Korean music, to appreciate the inimitable sound of a female Korean traditional music voice. "How do they make their voices like that?" I asked Jae-dal.

"I heard they eat tongue."

"Beef tongue?"

"Human tongue."

Object of envy. Countesses drink the blood of young virgins. Witches fatten children and cook them in pots. Said, *They found him with only one kidney in a bathtub full of ice.* Said, *Ripped the baby from the mother's womb and left her there to die.* Or, *Kidnapped the child and acted as if she were the mother and no one was the wiser.* Or, *Became pregnant with the babies of generals, gifts for the generals' sterile wives.* Folk tale, fairy tale, urban legend—drink the milk, eat the ovum of another species, purchase the child of another—what have we reproduced—smooth white steel of the airplane's shell, our maternity.

—◦—

Today is Christmas Day in Korea, where it's a dating holiday for lovers. Couples walk arm in arm, eat dinner at Outback Steakhouse and Tony Roma's Ribs, and, if they don't stop at Krispy Kreme first, buy a boxed cake sold on the street to eat at home. Today is Christmas Eve in the place we call England the Superior Country and America the Beautiful Country and I wonder if my parents have thought of me, if Mom remembers me when she plays her Christmas piano CDs on the stereo. My sister says Mom and Dad are hosting Christmas for the extended family at their house, and that means Mom will have a new centerpiece on the dining room table and mini cocktail wieners warming in the slow cooker all day, and there will be a fruit punchbowl and cheesy mashed potatoes and cranberry sauce. My cousin and her husband will show up with the new baby and everyone will say who the baby looks like, and my uncles will drink beer out of cans and my aunts will stand in the kitchen most of the day, unless they have finally decided to use paper plates. Cousin Shad, the son my parents never had, has been gone for three years now and I'm sure they'll tell stories about him, about the time he shot that deer, or when he worked at the car dealership or the department store in Moorhead. Today is Christmas Eve in Minnesota, and all is quiet on the snow, even at state institutions like prisons and the state security hospital. Whether you are a new baby or a sex offender, we're all in time together and it's Christmas Day for everyone. I wonder if my stalker's mother goes to see her son, if she is alone, or if she spends the holiday with her other children, if she has them. I wonder if she is eating a good meal. I wonder if my stalker is talked about in his family, or if he was talked about once but then one Christmas, the whole family silently agreed to not ask anymore. If someone does ask *How's John?* how does his mother reply? If Shad's mom asks *How's Jane?* how does my mother reply? Does anyone, even my mother, know why I'm not there? Even in Seoul, underneath the red neon lights, it's Christmas, even without all the people and things that make it seem like Christmas, like tradition, like family. Even if we adoptees have found our Korean families, and even if we are invited to family events, and if our Korean families do celebrate Christmas, their celebrations are undoubtedly Korean Christmas—they don't really feel like Christmas-Christmas to us. Most often, we spend the holiday with each other. We gather together in the basement of the adoptee guesthouse, and the French adoptee chef cooks what we think is a real Christmas dinner. We ask who sent packages, received packages, who didn't. And if they received something from home, we ask, *Did you open it yet?*

Although we lost it, spent it, and gave so much of it away, we still want to believe that time can make everything heal. Yet traumatic memory is trapped in time, always occurring in the present tense, its syntax *object, object, object.* Car, phone, gun. Cement floor, fluorescent overhead lights, boiler room. Wheelchair, candy bar, chocolate stains. *Floor, lights, chair, candy, stain. Object, object, object.*

If meaning is contained in the objects of our lives, to make sense of all these things is an act of the imagination and psychic survival. And if we use our imaginations to also make sense of the artifacts of someone else's life—the newspaper clippings, the police records and court judgments, the church brochures and the applications, the objects in the basement piled up to the ceiling, the false birth certificates and false identity papers that they had the government make to erase me and re-create me, because they believed they loved me—then this act of assemblage is also an act of compassion.

> ... *She told the investigator her son had left her home in the Twin Cities eleven days earlier, and said good-bye to everyone, as though he were not coming back ...*

> ... *Mr. Everett took the first train east and it will be some time before he returns.*

> "... *Eonje miguke dolaolkoyeyo?*" When will you return to America?

In a police interrogation, my stalker had referred to me, saying, "Who does she think she is, she's no better than me."

I was his obsession, and then he turned into mine. With the reality of his crime behind me, I brought what I knew of him with me to Korea, in a thick manila envelope. Since I met him in person only three times in my life, my knowledge of him is contained in the papers of his crime—the police reports, the newspaper clippings, the reports by forensic psychologists. His father died when he was two years of age; his mother was institutionalized for depression for a year following his father's death; he lived with grandparents during that time. The list continues: three stepfathers from six years old; witnessed violence against mother during marriage of mother to first stepfather; verbally abused by last stepfather; history of alcohol abuse on father's side. The difference is that in his early twenties, he took a trip to the White Earth Indian Reservation, and I took a trip to Korea.

Perhaps the evolution of his personality and his crime began with the same root as my depression, and in the end, the results—whether locking him up for his violence, or locking me up for my sadness—were the same.

A few Christmases ago, I had sent my photo to the female prison guard whom John had also stalked. She was shocked, remarking that at the time he stalked us, we looked very similar. At the time, we were both petite and had long, black hair.

Until I moved to Korea, the Victims and Witnesses office provided me with Polaroids of my stalker every time a hearing for his release came up. These days, from the safety of Korea, I look at him and his dark brown hair, his dark brown eyes, and his dark skin, and wonder what his mother looks like. I wonder what she looked like at the time his father died, when she was institutionalized, and when the two-year-old boy who would become my stalker—and who would nearly kill me—was handed off to his grandparents for a year. I wonder if he felt like an orphan. I wonder if at that time, his mother was also petite, and had long, black hair.

I was never especially close to Prokofiev the man ... I met Prokofiev in his music.

—Sviatoslav Richter, pianist

I met my stalker in the records of his crime, I met my Korean father's abuse in the fact of my adoption. My adoptive parents could have adopted anyone, and in my infant's need to be cared for and loved, I could have loved anyone. Strangers become lovers and then strangers again. What it is we mark upon each other: a death threat, an adoption, a kiss, a piece of music. Your song is marked upon me. Mine is marked upon you. This is the evidence we left, the palimpsest we share.

Well, it's Christmas again so Saint Lucia, take it easy on the hairspray. Saint Nick, we've been as good as we could under the circumstances. Saint Francis, please protect the pets and the lost dogs, especially in

Korea. Saint Christopher, protect us travelers. Who's in charge of lost objects, lost records, I don't remember. Who protects us from thievery, I never learned. Saint Mary, forgive us for that which we have mistranslated, that which we have broken, and that which we saw, but too late. We are all still searching for our mothers' faces. Our mothers are still searching for ours. May we all find each other someday.

Con una Dolce Lentezza

When I hear the sound of the piano, I know, without seeing, whether the keys that are played are black or white. Even without seeing a grand piano for a year, imprinted in my mind's eye is the way the light glints off the brass strings, the dull shine of pedals that are used every day and loved, the way even stockinged feet can wear down metal after years of music, the way running water or the wind can wear down stones. Even without ever having seen the inside of my parents' new house, I know how it looks because I know them that well. I know my mother's logic of where to store things, how to hang pictures, how to hide pictures, how to keep house, how things ought to be.

Here I've built a little house and all the walls are square. See the brand-new kitchen, the cabinets that don't need washing. There's a window over the sink, but you also have a dishwasher underneath the countertop. There's a garden in the back where you can grow your tomatoes. You always dreamed of a two-story house, so why don't you walk over there and try out the elevator. The basement is clean. The furnace never breaks. Don't worry about the roof because it's brand-new. There are no ghosts here because everyone is exactly who they are meant to be.

Even without ever having seen it, I can imagine the smooth shine of brass on a bullet meant for me, the object of a criminal's unrequited and racial love; I can imagine the body of the Chinese woman that has replaced mine in the bed of my former husband, the body of the Filipina woman that has replaced mine in the bed of another I almost married ten years ago. In the countryside of Korea, I can imagine the poor Vietnamese and poor Cambodian women who are advertised in bus shelters as able to immigrate and marry comparatively rich Korean farmers in less than three weeks, those farmers whom Korean women will not marry because they can marry comparatively even richer Western English teachers and gamble on the chance to go to the U.S., Canada, or Australia. No one says it's right, but that's the pecking order and we know it. I met a Chinese woman who supports her entire family by teaching English in China, but whose English is a little strange because she has never traveled to an English-speaking country. She helps facilitate adoptions of Chinese babies by Americans because she wants to "give them a chance to be American." I can imagine what she imagines.

These are what we call occasions for love.

When I dream of America I dream of my American parents. I dream we are sitting in a nearly abandoned restaurant somewhere in the Great Plains of the Midwest, with a parking lot outside where we park our car because we've been traveling. Outside, the restaurant looks like any cheap Korean fast-food place, but inside it looks more like an old wood-paneled American diner, the hot roast beef sandwich kind, and the menu board that is outside—full of Korean dishes like kimbap and chigae—has almost nothing on it when we see the same menu board inside. The waitress is a blond woman but I don't know if I should speak to her in English or Korean, so I don't speak at all. I want to explain all the Korean food to my parents and offer to go and look at the menu on the outside of the building again, but they just want doughnuts. They go right ahead and order in English. I dream of stacks of phone bills, eight hundred dollars' worth, which have somehow accumulated even though no one ever answered the phone. I dream of bad connections, lost connections; I watch them happen in real life; why do I need to dream. Every summer on every adoption-agency-run Motherland tour, busloads of adoptees visit orphanages and unwed mothers' homes, as if those orphans could be us, as if those women could be our mothers, as if we are supposed to find some comfort in the fact that we are all outcasts or missing persons to someone. I stay away from these spectacles of pity and mutual misery, yet when curious Korean people ask me about myself, I try to answer their questions simply but honestly. "Yes, I like Korea." "No, I'm not married." "Yes, I found my family." But, "No, I don't see my mother. She passed away." This phrase is one I know how to say in exactly the right Korean expression. It translates literally as, "My mother returned." Even more literally: "My mother turned around and went back." I add the honorific grammar in speaking about the dead. And when it comes out like that, in perfect Korean, in Korean that respects one's mother, ajummas touch my arm, gauging the health and girth of my flesh as my own mother had done. My wrist, in any hand, is thin. My skin, next to almost any other Korean's, is pale. The ajummas offer to bring me kimchi. They pity me, a motherless child finally become a real orphan, one with thin wrists and pale skin. What can they do but volunteer their own motherhood? "You can call me mama," they say, as if anyone can just take another's child, as if anyone can be a mother just because she wants to. But I don't need more adopting. *Your sentiments are very nice,* I don't say. *But you are not my mother.*

Even though our experiences of love have been tainted by pity, violence, money, naive fantasies, greed, and prejudice, we still search for connection. If there was ever such a thing as pure love, it must be the love between a mother and her child. If we were robbed of even that, then maybe we will always wander like hungry ghosts, gorging until vomiting, never able to be satisfied. Isn't it amazing that my sister has worked in a psychiatric hospital for nearly fifteen years, and for over a decade I have managed to stay on the outside of the walls of her workplace, only once embarrassing her inside with my presence, with my utter despair and emptiness? Isn't it fascinating that of the adopted Korean siblings of the adoptees who live in Seoul, about half of the siblings who live in the adoptive countries claim to care little or nothing about Korea, and the other half are in jail or in mental hospitals?

Isn't it a wonder that in Denmark 40 percent of all mental institution inmates are people of color—not ethnic Danes—and despite this, it is the people, not the society, who are called crazy?

Praise God that we are still alive despite this. Praise God that we still have the strength to try. Praise God that music also wants to return to where it began, its own origin, its center. And one of the first things we learn about Korean culture—when we learn the words for east, west, north, and south—is that center is also a direction. I was born of one mother and one father and this is indisputably true. So at my own center—this body made by a Korean woman and nourished from her own, this body from which all my thought and emotion arise, this body that is proof to the world that my birth mother existed on this earth, this one thing I know is real and that is indisputably my own—I make a small mark, and begin to chart a commonography of souls.

Chapter Eight

Presto Agitatissimo e Molto Accentuato

MANUAL OF INDUSTRIAL AND OCCUPATIONAL THERAPY
STATE HOSPITAL, ST. PETER, MINNESOTA

In assigning patients to jobs or tasks in a mental institution, careful consideration must ALSO be given to Environmental Factors. Can the patient work successfully under all or just some of the following factors?

1. Sudden change of temperature
2. Outside—Fair Weather Only
3. Outside—All Weather
4. Inside Only
5. Working With Others
6. Working Around Others
7. Fast Work
8. Repetitive Work
9. Competitive Work
10. Exacting Performance
11. Frequent Interruptions
12. Adequate Lighting
13. Adequate Ventilation
14. Electrical Hazards
15. High Places
16. Hazardous Machinery
17. Moving Objects
18. Cramped Quarters
19. Hot
20. Cold
21. Wet
22. Humid
23. Dry
24. Dusty
25. Slippery Floors
26. Toxic Conditions
27. Noise

In resettling in one's own country, careful consideration must ALSO be given to [internal and external] Environmental Factors. Can the immigrant work successfully all or just some ... what is possible ... what is the state of decay ... how advanced the illusion ... Try to immigrate at least TWICE in your life ... Do it without your Family ... Live where you Can ... learn

How to be Alone . . . steal if you Have To. Steal Love, steal Time, jump the Subway, go to Buffets and Take Things to eat Later, eat food First and drink water Last, never leave an embassy party without a bottle of Wine under your coat, cheat the Movie theater, develop an ethics of theft because even gangs have rules; thought must be given to what you will do if you are Interrupted while performing the aforementioned acts; while sharing a room the Quarters are Cramped but that is the price of sleeping for free; try not to be seen while using the bathroom; this lifestyle is Hazardous could be toxic so please remember, give Careful Consideration when assigning this job or task . . .

What parable, what catechism, could have prepared us for that which no one predicted would ever come to pass?

Our privilege is that if we wanted, we could go back to jobs or school, communities that are familiar, families that are familiar, countries where we can understand and be understood, countries where we don't have to figure out every detail anew, as if we were all eighteen years old again, trying to handle each burdensome facet of adult living—how to pay a bill, how to get phone service, how to get a driver's license, how to get insurance, how to register a new address with the government, how to pay taxes, how to get medical treatment, how to read something you got in the mail that looks like it might be important—all in a language we have forgotten, in a country where we have to explain ourselves even more than we had to in our adoptive countries. As a community we have a collective memory of the unfortunate dealings of adult Korean adoptees with Korean nationals within the recent past, so as a community we are wisely distrustful and dependent upon a network of people who won't take advantage of our obvious vulnerability. My elder sister had told me before even the adoptees told me: "Don't trust anyone," she said, "except our family. Watch out for bad people. You still cannot tell bad Koreans from good Koreans." It makes our world small. We don't have to live like this; we specifically were *not* supposed to live like this. It would probably make things easier for everyone involved if we would just go back.

But as seasons unexpectedly become years, as taxes go delinquent in our adoptive countries, causing us to wonder whether we can ever go back even if we wanted to, and state IDs and credit cards expire and occasional visits back to adoptive countries become more and more infrequent, we adoptees—for whom so much has been decided by chance, and for whom one of our only collective truths is that we were born as Koreans in Korea—live as immigrants among other immigrants. We have learned that in a boardinghouse, when shoes disappear, it's because someone borrowed them. Wait a while and the shoes will turn up again. In the meantime, borrow someone else's; shoes are not private property. Same goes for umbrellas. Depending on your friends, money and sleeping rooms might also be communal property, especially if you have friends who are hungry or homeless. Cheap ramen, developed as a postwar alternative to rice, is a blessing. For peace of mind, we have learned to assume that everything is OK until it's not. We have learned that, illiterate or not, the signing of contracts is inevitable. Follow the rules you know and make up the rest. Those who cannot tolerate life without fairness, order, reliable payment, or kept appointments don't last long here. Those who have lasted longer assess the realities: that in one of the world's largest cities, our community is too small to avoid ex-boyfriends and ex-girlfriends and others we'd rather not see, and we learn to navigate a society that is (with our own adoptions as proof) unsympathetic to vulnerable people, judgmental about difference, and hostile to outsiders.

Our collective homesickness is for the three things that all immigrants miss: family, friends, food. We find ways to cope: the warm feeling in your stomach that you have after Thanksgiving dinner can be simulated by a Lotte bulgogi burger. Friendship can be simulated by having a lot of acquaintances. Real acceptance can be simulated by superficial acceptance and romantic bulimia. Psychological services— the same ones that never worked in our adoptive countries anyway— can be simulated by passing time with simulated friends and a real bottle of soju.

I look at the summer photos and realize that, come September, of all the happy faces in the picture, only a fraction remain in Seoul. The rest went back. Each June is *hello hello hello;* each late August is *good-bye good-bye good-bye:* Seoul is an endlessly revolving door of people for whom true intimacy and trust are so difficult to achieve. But if and when we can feel close to someone, it's so hard to say good-bye. So with whatever capacity we still have to love and to trust, we say *Hello good-bye hello good-bye very nice to meet you, how it hurts me to say good-bye.* When Bad Dominique is obviously being poisoned at the table— by alcohol and despair—and a summer vacationer fills his glass yet again and raises it with a cheerful *"Konbae!"* the one who says, "Stop, don't let him drink more, can't you see he's had enough?" is the one who looks crazy. The one who calls friends and asks if they've seen a depressed adoptee who seems to have disappeared for several days is the one who is called controlling. Me, the one who, screaming, pulls him out of the driver's seat of a car he is about to steal, is the one who's called hysterical. "It's not alcoholism. It's lack of cannabis," claim the French.

Although we have traveled oceans and spent all our money just to be together, this is a sad and empty kind of togetherness when everything's cool, it's all OK, everyone can make their own choices and it's not anyone else's problem or responsibility, nothing matters. When the next suicide attempt arises, nobody is shocked and people actually laugh; this is a community where nearly everyone has either made a suicide attempt or knows someone who has, where almost everyone knows what that place feels like—the place where you don't really want to die but you do want to stop being hurt and lonely and you don't know how to go about doing that. If he wants to die, then he should go ahead and die, but don't bother everyone about it for months and months, the adoptees said. "Tell him he should take more pills," one advised.

Why is putting depressed people together with other depressed people supposed to help? A European friend assured me that locking people up for being sad—dangerously sad—is an American thing. In my early twenties, upon approval of my discharge from a psychiatric unit, I talked to a new admit for about an hour before I was picked up from the hospital. In that lung-colored smoking lounge, his dangerous sadness made perfect sense to me. He made more sense to me than the psych techs who doled out useless cheerleading squad self-help advice to incest survivors, bulimics, and adoptees: "Cheer up!" or "Get over it!" or "Stop feeling sorry for yourself!" I had wondered what was wrong with *them*. At the time, and often even now, someone who is considered sick—who has allowed himself to feel the experience of human life deeply and that is the reason for his suffering—makes sense to me. Actually, every patient I have ever met in a psychiatric unit has made pretty good sense to me. And the friendliest Koreans I have ever met—with no qualms or obvious embarrassment about talking to me in my broken Korean, because they are actually trying to communicate and words are only a small part of that—have been mentally handicapped.

(Tip: If you ever find yourself perfectly melancholy and in a psychiatric unit, but don't want to stay there and make new friends, when the workers ask, "Do you fantasize about suicide?" tell them "NO!" But if you slip up and say "Yes," when they ask, "Do you have a plan?" give them a very resounding "NO WAY!" That might be lying, but I think we have already established the convenience and usefulness of being a liar in certain situations.)

Greetings, Friends, from the province of Gyeonggi. I have tried to make a home for myself in Korea over the past four years. During this time, I have lived in the cities of Seoul, Nonsan, and Gimhae, and I have traveled to many other places throughout this country. I have seen the most intimate aspects of Korean family life. I have seen things that no tourist will ever see even though I am still in many respects a tourist. I have been welcomed in my mother's village, have learned enough Korean language and culture to get by. I will not starve here for want of food. I have observed that of all the opportunities that transnational adoption gave me, gave us, the one opportunity we were not given was the chance to be an ordinary Korean person: an ordinary shopkeeper, an ordinary day laborer, an ordinary student or husband or wife. Because of this I have consciously decided not to try to assimilate; I cannot do it twice in one lifetime. During my time on the margins of Korean society, I have lived among others who also cannot undo what has already been done to them. I have lived among the bravest of people who also found no reason to pass for anyone but who they already are. Of these people, I wish to bear witness.

So let this be a testament for an adoptee I loved, whose father was an ajeossi with a shiny scar beneath his forearm tattoo, and who put on his best black jacket with yellow gold buttons, and came to the very same building where he had left his infant son twenty-eight years before. At the adoption agency overlooking the Han River, he beheld the face of his lost son, but all he could see, all he could talk about, was the woman who was the mother. *He looks like his mother, his face resembles hers so much.* He didn't bother to ask his son what he had made of his life during all those years, all those years in which he had entrusted his only son's life to strangers, or what his son's adoptive parents were like, or if he even had siblings in his adoptive family, or if he had gotten an education—because all he could think about was the woman he still loved, despite his current marriage, absent current wife, and two present daughters. He wanted to eat meat and drink soju with this woman again, whom he had loved but never married, and live together as a family. When this news reached the mother's ears, she did not appear to hate the father as much as her sister and her mother still did. Maybe she loved him once. She had applied makeup to meet her son. Her red lips turned down a little; her eyebrows drew together over the blue eye shadow. The colors were wrong for her face, gaudy, giving the impression that she had borrowed the makeup from someone else for the special occasion. She had applied the makeup clumsily, like someone who worked every day from morning until night in a cheap restaurant and normally didn't have time to make herself up. Over the months, in her sadness and confusion, she thought about but failed to call the son who searched halfway around the world for her, who lived in a foreign country for three years just to find her. Due to the circumstances—she had another son by another husband—the son was not allowed to call her. The adopted son got sick of being the source of everybody else's shame. So he convinced himself that his mother hated him while he was in the womb, and he didn't want to see the bitch who gave birth to him like an animal anyway. The father could call the son, because he was the father and Korean fathers can do what they want. And when he called the son late at night or very early in the morning, the son stopped answering the phone; after his father had been jailed for drunk driving and the son could recognize the father's drunkenness even in a different language, hearing the greeting of *"Ahdel!"* "Son!" over the phone was less appealing than it had been in the beginning. Finally the father stopped calling altogether. In the end, the son went on as if he had never found his parents, justifying his own drunkenness and destruction with the broken lives of his parents, aborting two of his own children, using his own lovers for what he could get—a place to sleep, sex, money. He never knew his real name because his father remembered it was one name, Hyun-su, and his mother remembered another, Min-su. So he continued to use his French name, Dominique, and I learned to call him that when I wanted to reach his heart, although I never could.

And so, over the next two years, he sporadically came in and out of my life, with all his drunkenness, the phone calls throughout the night, the pounding on the door at five o'clock in the morning and the complaints of the neighbors—*"Do you want me to call the police?"*—the three- or four-day binges on alcohol Eastern and Western, his sincere and passing regret, my own reactions that turned me into someone also unreliable, also crazy, also embarrassingly and obviously "co-dependent." I scolded myself for not just giving up on him, but I also wondered what would be wrong with my humanity if I did. So came forth the almost eternal hope: *This time, he'll quit drinking. This time, he really means it.* Inevitably, disappointment followed in a week, again in another week, and again and again until I felt the physical and emotional exhaustion that comes from loving an alcoholic. Not just from loving an alcoholic, but from loving an alcoholic in Korea—a country where a medical doctor can actually see the liver damage glowing on a twenty-eight-year-old through an ultrasound, and still fail to say the word "alcoholic." From loving an alcoholic adoptee in Seoul—an environment that condones addiction because Korea is not a country where people entertain inside their homes, but Korea *is* a country that has a highly ritualized drinking culture and at least we can imitate that, so when adoptees go out, we go to bars, and everyone else is drinking, and there's always a new vacationer, a new drinking buddy, or a friend who has just returned from Europe or China with marijuana or opium. Even so, I allowed Dominique to mark his story deeply into me, like a cut that I needed, just as my mother allowed my father to mark his story deeply into her, and into her children. I didn't want to repeat my own Korean mother's mistakes, but in some way I had to rework my history. I was trying to get the ending right. And I was trying to recover my father. I was trying to recover the dead. In that season of awakening I found a piece of understanding for my mother, and for my father's tortured and self-hating heart.

"What is the reality?" Dominique asked me after we had gone to his adoption agency together for the first time to search for his mother. His social history of abandonment and orphanhood that day, as interpreted by the social worker, was different than it had been the last time he had gone to the agency. The same file, the same life, would be reinterpreted over the years again and again. "All I know is that I am alive," Dominique said, "and I am with you."

Although he had at one time saved his writing, Dominique took the habit of writing a few pages and then ripping them out and throwing them into the wastebasket. Every day he started a new diary. His reality became the sum of his story in the present, because there was only the present. There used to be a past and he had saved it in a newspaper clipping, the one that had made him into an adoptee celebrity for one day, the brave and mighty adoptee who, out of principle, went to jail for a month for a visa violation because he refused to be labeled a "foreigner." But then there was the less distant past, the part where I stood in the Seoul Immigration Office with him because he decided to renew his visa so he could work, and I realized as he stood staring at that one piece of paper with confusion on his face that *he couldn't read the fucking form.* He had let his visa lapse because he had to fill out the form and he couldn't read it, because it's all in English and Korean, and he reads French and he was too proud to be accompanied by a volunteer from any of the adoptee service groups who could have actually helped him. I couldn't blame him for being proud.

Proud men have to struggle for themselves, so that is why whatever they can manage has to be good enough. At times the most fragile of creatures, men who hate themselves try to drink their courage, like Dominique, like my Korean father. I asked my younger Korean sister if she hated him while she was growing up, and she said, "No, I just feared him." My father's story, I will never fully know. I don't want to make my sisters cry every time I see them, asking about the past that they have tried so hard to forget. Every time my sister stands at the kitchen sink of her large and expensive apartment, provided by her husband, she can see the village of the poor snaking high up the opposite mountain, so that every time she does the dishes she can see her past. Why do I want to remind her even more of her childhood, to ask every detail about the father I never met? I asked just once if our mother ever loved our father. My sisters argued over the question. My older sister said no. My younger sister, who had one day announced in English, "I often feel lonely," said that our mother loved him.

I had thought that I loved Dominique, but maybe it was only desperation and my own need to be loved. Somehow I must have thought that if he needed me, he couldn't leave me. Could I buy love from him in the same way my parents tried to buy it from me? Why do people think that orphans want their lives changed? Why did I think that I could have the satisfaction of changing Dominique's life, whether or not we were equally pitiable orphans? I kept hoping for things to change and they never did. I kept hoping for a future and it never happened.

Over and over Dominique had said to me, "I just want destruct everything." I had hoped that someday Dominique would save his pages, instead of writing his life and then throwing it away. He had left his notebooks and photographs at my house, his clothes at a boarding-house, his clothes in a subway locker, little souvenirs of himself scattered around Korea. After he made off with a month's worth of my salary, he sent me an e-mail, not telling me where he was, but saying he wanted to start a new life. I thought that if one month's salary would buy him a new life, that would be a bargain. But I knew it wouldn't, and it didn't.

I loved him in a peculiar way—part mother, part sister, part friend, part lover, part frustrated do-gooder. He brought out the absolute worst in me, and also the best, despite that whatever we had between us in the end mattered not at all.

The futility of love, the indifference of the world, and the responsibility of freedom are the three things I learned from watching Dominique's life. He taught me that we all have the freedom to destroy ourselves. But, even though I suspect that living is not his ultimate goal, I hope Dominique will be able to survive his own life, and then reinterpret it in whatever way will pull his shattered existence back together in a way that is, to him, worth the struggle. And in the end I hope he will make something meaningful out of his life, whatever that idea means to him. I believe we all have the power to do that.

Chapter Nine

—◄o►—

Coda

약: 藥: medicine

악: 樂: music

음악: 音樂: (sound + music): music

음절: 音節: (sound + joint): syllable

자음: 子音: (child + sound): consonant

모음: 母音: (mother + sound): vowel

악구: 樂句: (music + phrase): a clause; a phrase;
   a section; a sentence

The sound of piano music comes through the open window of a boardinghouse room. Mix with the night sounds of the street, rain on metal rooftops and pavement, another season passed. Rain and hot, rain and cool, rain. *"Naeil bwayo,"* students shout, "See you tomorrow." Click of women's heels as they pass the boardinghouse with their lovers. Seoul accent, distinct sound, pretty-faced girls with blisters on their feet, high laughter, tops of umbrellas like wet black mushrooms. The white walls of the room faintly reflect Motel Daisy's neon sign flashing all night; the lights run bottom to top in a flashing rainbow. *Well Come.* The sound of a car's tires as it passes on the street, *whoosh* and *whirr.* From inside rooms comes the sound of Japanese-accented Korean, the laughter of the Korean man watching TV alone. Clink of rice bowls and chopsticks against the sink as the ajumma washes the dishes, singing. I recognize some of the melodies, the old Korean love songs my mother would have known, *dangshineun, dangshineun,* you, you.

I remember every piano I have ever known, like every lover I have ever touched with my hands, the texture of their keys and the sound of their voices, tension and release of this music, those I have held in my arms, dangshineun. Music holds the symmetrical grief of women who loved men who loved alcohol but hated themselves, of mothers whose sons are criminals, whose sons were good ol' boys, whose sons were never born, whose daughters returned but too late. In this strike of hammer followed by the curve of dying sound lie calculations of trueness and calculations of the missing, and what I must hold inside my heart at once: harmony and dissonance, the expected and the un-expected, the ignited and the extinguished, and these syllables I long to be marked deep with, let me hold them inside my mouth:

Birthmark:

Language of my lost memory

Language of my lost mother

Language my mother dreamed in

Language she conceived me in

Language I am desperate to speak, ache to shape, drop the jaw, open the throat, say the words that feed you first: rice, sweet potato, persimmon; and the simple words for people next: *namja, yoja, neo, na.* Link sounds together and you can speak, link patterns of sound, patterns of loving, patterns of history, patterns of grammar, patterns of speech, of thought, of understanding, give me syllable, give me con-sonant and vowel, phrase and sentence, mother sound, child sound, joined sound, mother give me voice . . .

Lento, Irrealmente

Irrealmente. If I were writing fiction, I'd write that I have been on a long journey back to where I came from, that I am making a historical cor-rection within my own life, that thirteen years and six trips to Korea later, I'm fully integrated into Korean society. I came back to my roots and I speak Korean fluently, can detect all the nuanced and circular meanings of other Koreans, love to eat kimchi even for breakfast, mar-ried a Korean man, made Korean babies. I'd write that we live in Seoul because that's where the best schools and private academies are. My husband works for Samsung, we live in a peach-and-beige apartment high-rise along with a thousand neighbors, and I am a homemaker in an apartment that is identical to the apartments of all my friends:

the veranda with the potted plants and clothing rack in front, the veranda in the back for cooking fish, and all the accoutrements: kimchi refrigerator, cherry wood trim in the living room, the bathroom's unused bathtub and heated toilet seat, Western beds. I take an interest in yoga, swimming at the pool with goggles and cap, hiking in a red shirt and mountain boots, bicycling with gloves and helmet. Sometimes I take classes with my housewife friends to learn to sew or cook French food. I watch Korean dramas while I clean vegetables for dinner. I'll start my kids on flash cards before they can sit up; I'll send them to private kindergarten and then an international school; in middle school they'll study until midnight, and after they graduate from high school, if they don't get into Seoul National University, I'll send them to school in America. After they graduate from university, I hope they will either be teachers or government workers. I call my sisters every day and we chat about domestic life and we meet for lunch once a month on Sundays; I call my brother less often but drive down with my sisters to see him once or twice a year. When we take family vacations, we go on package tours that promise one Korean meal a day, even in Thailand. My husband and I are thinking of going to Australia to live when we reach old age because their social welfare is better, or maybe we can retire in the Philippines. I go to church every Sunday and play piano for the choir. I have no conflict in my family because I have turned completely Korean, as if I never left, or maybe only studied abroad. But that is a fiction.

A true story: she had never seen her next-door neighbor in the building of one-room apartments, but from the shoes left next to the outer door, she knew that he had large feet. Twice, a woman with a shrill and demanding voice came to his room and yelled. He didn't yell back. After that she didn't return. Usually he was alone. Occasionally he smoked cigarettes and the smoke wound through the vent and into her adjacent bathroom. Even less occasionally, he cooked and the smell of fish frying in oil drifted out onto his veranda and drifted back in through her windows. Every night around 1:00 a.m., he took a quick, practical shower. He always turned on the water to warm first, and the water made sounds of falling onto the tile floor before it made the sounds of falling onto his body, the sounds of soaping, scrubbing, rinsing, clearing the throat. He slept on the opposite side of the same wall that she slept against in her adjacent room, and at night, when she placed her head next to his without his knowing, she could hear his breath rising and falling. Even though she had never seen him, and never knew his name, this small intimacy from the other side of the wall was comforting.

In college she had learned that (') is the mark used by musicians to indicate a breath, that when playing in ensemble, breathing together is fundamental, as it is in Tantric lovemaking. She also learned that the iambic pentameter is the length of the human breath, that God breathed his life force into Adam, that if she should ever give birth to a child, she could control her waves of pain with breath. From her mother, who had never given birth to a child, she learned that an in-haled breath, unreleased, meant disapproval, or worse yet, it meant she wanted to say something but also did not want to hear her daughter's reply. In fact, she was afraid of the daughter's reply. That was because the daughter wouldn't have minded an all-out fight (in Korean drama style, though she didn't know that yet), and preferred yelling to not breathing. The daughter wanted to slap her mother on the back, force her to breathe. If she had done that, maybe she could have forced her mother back into feeling sensations of hunger, of desire, and even real anger. Instead the mother held her breath, drank between one and three Southern Comfort Manhattans before her one meal each day, and took pills for acid reflux, high blood pressure, and menopause. The daughter took pills for her emotions.

Enough was the word that ruled their lives. There was something like the anticipation of famine or a civil emergency. There could never be enough canned vegetables in bulk, instant seasoned rice pilaf by the bucket, or snack crackers in giant double boxes crammed into closets, cupboards, the basement. One could blame it on the mother's own parents, Depression-era dairy farmers who were absent because they were always in the barn, leaving the then young mother in the house to raise her younger brothers and sisters, though she was only a child herself. One could blame it on the mother's father, who had died hated by his daughters.

The mother's absent childhood spread throughout the house like a poisonous vapor. It was a gnawing hunger of insatiable want, not for food but something else. And so from an early age, the mother's daughter interpreted herself, too, as not enough: what someone would take if they couldn't get what they really wanted.

So when she became a young woman, the daughter took whoever would also take her in return—anyone who held both the promise of rescuing her from her self-loathing and also the promise of ultimately discarding her. Fetishists were a good match because they liked her not in spite of her defective Asian body, but because of it, and they did not care so much about her humanity. She found that her longest-lasting relationships were with men who had been abandoned emotionally or physically by a parent, whether through alcoholism or divorce, by having been shipped off to a grandparent during the summers, or having had parents who had not loved each other, but who had stayed in the marriage for the sake of the children. With these people she experienced the spark that felt like real love. The world, she learned, was full of grown-up children, all who had been abandoned in some way. They could look successful and "well adjusted" just like anyone else. Often they looked more successful than anyone else, able to reflect others' desires, motions and speech designed to lure, entice, deceive—as if being oneself would never be a good enough reason for anyone to love them.

Of my lost family, my American mother told me, "Get over it." Though I wanted a father, he said nothing to me—except that I would have liked his own father, who died before I was born. So those things that fathers often teach daughters—about money, savings, cars—I learned from my boss at work. My Korean father hated me when I was born, so, fatherless, I learned everything about how to behave toward older Korean men from strangers who pitied me. My Korean mother told me, *Marry a Korean man. Hurry.*

My adoption failed to mold me into a global citizen, a true cosmopolitan, a person who has accumulated the riches of culture and experience, marketable job skills. I will never be able to think like a Korean person, no matter how hard I study, no matter which language holds my thought. "When they adopted you they stole your mind," Dominique had told me matter-of-factly, as if he had understood this for years. In my heart's irrational math one Korea plus one America equals nothing—equals motherless, languageless, countryless. That is because my longing is fitting of the person I am—daughter of high school–educated, blue-collar Minnesotans, daughter of an uneducated Korean mother, a Korean construction site worker. I was not raised a social climber. My longing has always been exactly the same: I want love. I want to be safe. I want to go home. How these simple wishes have gone unfulfilled, how warped they have become as I have traveled through life seeking love, safety, and home from strangers, just as the moment I arrived an alien and daughter into the home of my American parents.

My Korea dreams and my America dreams begin to meld into one unending dream, placeless, detached from reality, superimposed upon each other: Korean words come out of my American mother's mouth; I am driving on the interstate that cuts through Minneapolis, except that it cuts through Seoul; I walk through the houses and neighborhoods of Minnesota that I have lived in while holding a book about Korea in my hand. In the place where my speech is not understood, but where I pass unnoticed as any other female on the street, I no longer have stalker nightmares, so I no longer wake up sweating and screaming. Nor do I have dreams of being chased through a maze, the ones that are my earliest memories. Maybe there are no more of those

terrifying dreams because the thing that was chasing me was Kor̨
that beast that failed to nurse her own children but sold them instead.
I went straight back into her belly, where she could no longer chase
me. I became a part of her again though I always was, even though my
adopted life was supposed to save me from being myself.

Despite all the things I was told were not real, that didn't matter,
that were not true, that would pass, what has always been true has
been the permanency of my loneliness, this defining characteristic
that I have grown like hair uncut since childhood. My loneliness has
grown like the morning glories of my mother's summer garden, each
year after a long hibernation reviving, filling out their old vines and
climbing farther, taller, and blooming wilder. Summer was the time to
seek aloneness, like the time spent on my bicycle pedaling west toward
Fargo. The grids of farmland green and gold now roll out in my imagination, and upon those grids of predictability, those straight and inter-
secting country roads, are the stoic suffering and disappointment of my
American parents. Each memory, each observation, could be observed
only because I was an observer, and this has been my deep and shining
aloneness—to watch as if on film an all-American family, my own, at
Christmas dinner together, and then as if on film a traditional Korean
family, my own, at Chuseok eating and laughing and talking together;
to observe, inside the clubs of Seoul, adoptees a decade younger than I
dancing together, all their differences blurred by hip-hop music, strong
alcohol, strobe lights pulsating through the cigarette darkness and the
late hour; to wait exactly twenty years after we no longer lived together,
on the occasion of her twentieth high school reunion, for my adopted
sister to admit that in all her teen popularity, she had felt disconnected.
"Acting. Survival," she said.

Who knows what is the genealogy of this familiar aloneness, the
austere restlessness, the floating despair—whether it is from the birth-
ing or the taking of the body, or the raising of it, or whether what is
so often interpreted as strength or independence or resilience is really
that, or just the lingering effects of an intimacy with violence. I would

like to say something about choice and freedom, but I am not sure what to say, under these circumstances. These are circumstances: the fact that I cannot imagine putting any four-and-a-half-year-old child that you have raised and loved on an airplane and sending her to a foreign country, yet my mother did it; the fact that I am sadder and angrier for my sister than I am for myself; the fact that my sister tells me to let go of my anger, no matter how I manage it; the fact that I am trying but I haven't managed yet; the fact of my homelessness in the country of which I hold my passport, the fact of Seoul, how I loathe its energy of destruction; how this destruction is inscribed into the face of almost every adoptee I meet after midnight; how I sometimes hate this country as much as I sometimes hate my own mothers, whom I also love intensely, and deeply, and maybe that is why we call Korea the Motherland.

We Koreans—whatever that means—have emerged from the disaster of the twentieth century, bumping and scratching our way into the next, disoriented and confused, not knowing the difference between stranger or family, friend or enemy. In less than one hundred years we have gone from a nation closed and hostile to Westerners to a nation that makes an offering of its own children to them. And the sparkling miracle upon the Han River that Seoul has become, with all its great wealth laid out upon the skyline, came to pass because of the endurance of many people. We—the outcasts—are numbered among them. And now to this place we have returned, a stain upon the conscience of Korea, straddling two centuries with our brokenhearted mothers, our guilt-ridden fathers. We took no vow of silence, nor did our families, yet still we can hardly speak.

So I delight in the simple and quiet life that Korea offers me: white towels drying on a rack outside a barbershop, each tiny loop of the terrycloth fabric casting its own shadow in the sun; the immediate sharp pull underneath my tongue when I taste kimchi chigae cooked with tuna oil; the smell of the Han River and flocks of sparrows flitting above the pumpkin fields next to it; the sound of bamboo leaves rustling in the wind on a mountain trail. Although I fantasize, when alone in the mountains, that in nature there is no question about my belonging in this land, that Mother Nature accepts me completely, without questioning my Koreanness or foreignness—it is also true that if I died there, nature would be completely indifferent. Nevertheless, the small details—knowing the names of plants, smelling the lotus blossoms in the spring at temples, finishing meals with burnt rice mixed with hot water—make life worth living here. Breathe the air, drink the water. Breathe in, breathe out, be nourished.

I love Korea because Korea has taught me how to be quiet and alone. I love Korea in the way that only someone who has fought to reclaim something can. I love Korea even though she didn't love me.

I love Korea when I'm eating mussels out of a copper pot with a friend, knocking back the soju one tiny glass cup after another. I love Korea when I'm at the fat ajeossi's restaurant eating bibimbap out of a sizzling hot stone bowl. I love Korea when I'm inside the walls of my small room alone, eating macaroni and cheese and American breakfast cereals. I love American *How are ya*s and that great American optimism and curiosity that so many adoptees bring with them. I love Korea best when I am on a great American road trip. I love to drive the highway measured in kilometers from sea to shining sea, up and down the peninsula, from the craggy, rocky mountains of Gangwando facing Japan to the flat sand beaches of the West Sea facing China, from Pocheon near North Korea to the hot, shipbuilding islands at the southern tip. I love the Korea of my mother, the hardscrabble, survivalist Korea of wild mountain vegetables that my sisters pick from around my mother's grave and take home to eat for dinner. I love the Korea of my friends, the Korea where kimchi is stashed inside the fridge, and salty black Danish candy is stashed on top of it. I love Korea when it smells of French bistro cooking and Belgian beer, thin Dutch caramel-filled waffles and coffee lattes. I love my Korea, where Buddhist monks call upon the power of the mountain to improve their pool and Ping-Pong games. I love the tiny, bridgeless island of Jebu-do, whose only access to the mainland is a tar road that seems to rise out of the West Sea twice a day during low tide, and seems to sink into the sea again as the tide rises. I love Korean village life, where inside every store my brother makes even the most minor purchase, he sits down for a cup of coffee or juice and chats with his friends, and after that he stands outside for a little while longer and talks to the villagers passing by on foot or tractor. I love countryside people because they are like the Koreans I have read about in books, renowned for their friendliness and their sense of slow time. How I love that slow life guided by the fields and the sun, that place where even strangers know that I am the sister of my brother. How I long to live near my brother someday as a normal villager, in the gohyang of my mother, even though I am quite sure I never will.

The questions Koreans ask me haven't changed despite eleven years of going back and forth to this country, despite how much I have learned, despite how hard I have tried to be accepted. "Can you say *Daehanminguk*?" "Do you like kimchi?" "Do you like Korean men?" "Can you sing 'Arirang'?" The abandoned singer of "Arirang," rejected at the mountain pass by her lover, sings that before the lover walks even ten *li* without her, a disease will come to his feet. For Korean people, being separated causes pain, causes aching. For Korean people, this song expresses what it means to be Korean. This is han. This is jeong. Korea, I know your song even better than you do. Why do you think you can leave the past behind?

I love Korea even though I have been stripped of the qualities Koreans think make a Korean. I love Korea because here I feel less hungry. I love Korea because here I feel less unsafe. I love Korea because here is my uncomfortable home. I love Korea despite my abiding grief. I love Korea because Korea is the place where I was born, and where all my ancestors were born, and where they died, and where I hope to die. I love Korea because I am Korean.

The only neat endings are the fake ones. The real stories are a never-ending balance sheet of cause and effect, sowing and reaping. So cut again to red red Seoul, this time to the Hotel Sofitel Ambassador, after the annual meeting of the adoptee-run service organization G.O.A'L., where for one night only nobody is drinking soju because the wine is free. The conversation in the hotel bar is the same as always: "Where do you come from?" "How long have you been here?" "Where do you work?" and "When are you going back?" We can spot, by ear, the ones who habitually lie to Koreans about where they grew up: American adoptees are not fooled by a Kentuckian who claims she grew up in New York; Danish adoptees are not fooled by a provincial adoptee who claims to have grown up in Copenhagen, and it seems that almost anyone who has done enough time in Seoul can hear the difference be-tween Belgian French and French French.

When the band starts up under the stage lights red, yellow, and blue, it's a Filipino band with three female singers wearing skirts too short, lingerie tops too skimpy, makeup too obvious. They remind me of the women in the glow of the meat lights in Yongsan, lined up be-hind glass in rows, their private rooms behind curtains. Selling them-selves in a different way than "the girls" in Yongsan, but likewise doing what they have to do, they sing American pop songs of the 1980s and contemporary Korean pop for their audience: adoptees able to be seen but not heard from the stage, who don't know the words to the Korean songs anyway.

But the songs that we know in English take us back. In his mind, my friend goes back to his days working in the Dutch shipyards, and suddenly he's driving to work again, windows open and cool salt sea breeze blowing on his face. He misses the cafés by the canals of Amsterdam, the coffee shops that sell hash, his ex-girlfriend, as beau-tiful when she woke up as when she went to sleep, now the mother of someone else's child. Another friend hears a song and she's in love again, remembering the night she first heard it, and the boy from art school who made her feel beautiful, who gave her a dream for a few months. And when the band plays "Summertime" in the style of Janis Joplin, I remember that in Joplin's incomparably expressive voice the whole world could hear the very spirit of her, what was indeed divine in her despite her immolated life, and through her music she let us peer into her heart in the same way that all music transports us through time and distance, opening our hearts further to each other and to ourselves, even in our unintended creation.

Here is the story of my creation: my grandmother fell dead of a heart attack when my mother was nine years old. My mother, the worthless youngest daughter of a house that already had both sons and cows, was married off to a poor house in a neighboring village. When her first husband died and she had to go to Seoul to earn money—the house of her mother-in-law had no grown men in it—she wanted to take her young son with her. But her son—the oldest grandson of the twenty-third generation of the oldest grandfather—belonged more to the house than to his mother. So she left him there, next to the mountain near his dead father and all his ancestors, to be raised by her mother-in-law, and occasionally came home from Seoul bearing chickens and shoes.

Doesn't a woman working in a big city need a man to protect her? And so I was born to my mother and her second husband on the street, the fifth worthless daughter of my sonless father. Later, my father put a blanket over my face to make me die. I refused. Later, I almost starved in the orphanage. Perhaps even then I would not take the nourishment of someone not my mother. But still I refused to die. Later, a stranger would plot my death. His plot remained only that.

I will waste neither my life nor my death. Death by my father's hand, by the gun of a rapist, or even the stink of hunger would have been meaningless. Even if I was thought to be worthless because of my gender, the accumulated suffering of Korean women has to be worth something. The relationship between a mother and daughter is worth something. Even loneliness can be worth something.

I had honed my loneliness at the piano, sixty minutes at a time, ninety minutes, four hours: an endless, deep, and abiding intimacy measured on a kitchen timer. Before I came to Korea, I sold the piano to another writer, the music books to a man with a canary and an angora cat. But the loneliness—that I brought that with me, to my first thousand days in Korea.

In those thousand days I have seen green pine trees, brilliant blue skies, the clear white bright lights of Apkujeong in the southern, hyper-modernized part of Seoul, and the unrestrained traditional colors of the palaces north of Seoul's Han River. Yet it is red—when I close my eyes and imagine Korea—that stands out in my mind: Go-Stop red, butcher shop red, water cannon red, hooker red, Jesus Loves All the Little Children red. And when I close my eyes and imagine Korea, despite the many places I have visited and the busyness of my life—my sixty-hour workweek surrounded by Korean colleagues, the company meals and the adoptee activist meetings, the nights of poker and clubbing with people from all over the world—the place that is most familiar to me is my own room, with its closed door. The closed door has moved from one building to another, one city to another, even as I have accumulated more books, more clothes, and even an electronic piano. But the loneliness behind each door of the first thousand nights has always been the same, the time always night, the season always rainy, water ever present in a country made up of only half a peninsula and a few hundred islands.

Over the West Sea that flows over the coast of both South and North Korea, my sisters scattered my father's ashes, returning him to the northern province from whence he came before the war. There is no mark left upon the world of this man, whose sonless family line was turned to ash along with his body. There is no mark of this man who tried to kill his fifth daughter, believing her worthless. But I am still living.

I have lived in Korea for a thousand days, and I would like to live in Korea for at least a thousand more. However those thousand days come, let them come. Let them be rainy, let them be snowy, let them be full of sunshine and smog. Let the typhoons and the yellow dust storms rage and cease, rage and cease. Let my days be filled with the people who are my own, no matter how hurt, how complex, how simple. Let my nights end breathing in harmony with a man whom I have never seen, but whose habits I know, and who sleeps on the opposite side of the wall. If loneliness has chosen me as its bride, let it have me. In my loneliness, let me be whole. In my loneliness, let me be human. Let me believe in the humanity of other people. Let them believe in mine. Let my spirit not be extinguished.

In the landscape of piano keys, the fugitive visions of the present become the past, reflected again into the reality of the present. But no matter what our past, our differences, our failures or achievements, we will all arrive alone and together at the end: the musicians, the poets, the factory workers; the dangerous insane, the assassins, and the slain; the good-hearted, the well-meaning, the profiteers and depraved; the mothers, the children, the indefinable, *uri,* we. *We are fearfully and wonderfully made,* we denizens of a single future fashioned by our own words, by our own hands—and in that time that is yet to come, our work can be just, forgiving, truthful, and abundant.

I know that full well.

Notes

The title of the book is derived from *Visions Fugitives, Op. 22* by Sergei Prokofiev, a set of twenty short, loosely related piano pieces that are often performed only partially or out of order. The composer took his title from the Russian poet Konstantin Balmont, whose poem *"mimolyotnosti"* translates from the original Russian into French as *"visions fugitives."* The translation used in the epigraph is found in David Nice's *Prokofiev: From Russia to the West 1891–1935.*

Quotations in Chapter One are from *Patterns of Relating: An Adult Attachment Perspective* by Malcolm L. West and Adrienne E. Sheldon-Keller and *Becoming Attached: First Relationships and How They Shape Our Capacity to Love* by Robert Karen, Ph.D.

In addition, the Korean sentence that translates as "Mother, I miss you" or more literally—"Mother, I want to see you"—points to the second photograph in Theresa Hak Kyung Cha's *Dictee,* which also includes the sentences "I want to go to my (ancestral) hometown" and "I am hungry"—or more literally—"My stomach is empty."

Quotations in Chapter Two are from the *St. Paul Pioneer Press* and *Playing in the Dark: Whiteness and the Literary Imagination* by Toni Morrison.

Documents about and from the hospital in St. Peter, Minnesota, can be found at the Southern Minnesota Historical Center's Manuscript Collection at Mankato State University's Memorial Library.

Quotations in Chapter Four are from *Quick and Easy Korean for Migrant Workers* by Jang Mal-hee and Park Myoung-sook. Other found text is apparently from a training manual of the U.S. Defense Department.

Excerpts of Prokofiev's memoirs in Chapters Three and Four are from *Sergei Prokofiev: Autobiography, Articles, Reminiscences,* edited by S. Shlifstein and translated by Rose Prokofieva.

The quote in Chapter Seven from the pianist Sviatoslav Richter is from *Sergei Prokofiev: A Biography* by Harlow Robinson.

All names, except the author's, have been changed.

Acknowledgments

Since the "end" of the Korean War, up to two hundred thousand South Korean children—both documented and undocumented by the Seoul government—have been sent as legal "orphans" to Western countries for the purposes of adoption, with the U.S., France, and the Scandinavian countries having received the majority of those children. The purpose of sending children from East to West was to give them "better lives," and the paperwork that made those adoptions possible was designed to give the children a "clean break."

So it was quite a surprise when, after the South Korean military dictatorships ended in the late 1980s, internationally adopted Koreans began voluntarily leaving their adoptive countries and returning to Korea. At the time this book was written (2004–2008), an estimated two hundred internationally adopted Koreans were active in the "adoptee community" in Korea, according to the adoptee-run service organization Global Overseas Adoptees' Link (G.O.A'L).

To my adopted Korean friends who left families, countries, languages, and cultures to meet the unknown in Korea—I offer my thanks for the privilege of witnessing a part of your lives. To those who came to Korea up to two decades ago, paving the way for those of us who live in Korea now, I offer my gratitude for your bravery and endurance. And to the over 1,364 Korean children who were sent overseas for adoption in 2007, and all the adoptees who are bound together only by the seemingly inconsequential yet permanent fact that we were sent so far from where we were born, I offer my hopes that someday, we will all find what we are searching for.

My heartfelt thanks to all those who helped with the development of this book, including the patient and kind staff at Graywolf Press, especially editors Fiona McCrae and Anne Czarniecki. In addition, Anna Ghosh of Scovil Galen Ghosh Literary Agency and Shannon Pennefeather helped get the book from proposal to print. Time to write was given through generous support from the Loft Career Initiative

Grant and the Loft-McKnight Artist Fellowship. As always, I am indebted to the professors of the English and music departments of Augsburg College in Minneapolis, who offered opportunities for intellectual and artistic exploration. In particular, pianist Jill Dawe allowed me to accompany my performance of *Visions Fugitives* with short prose poems printed inside the program, which over a decade later became parts of this book. John Mitchell (1940–2006) taught a class in contemporary American poetry, which eventually inspired those prose poems. Sun Yung Shin, who was writing *Skirt Full of Black* while I was writing this book, influenced me tremendously, as well as the many others who worked on *Outsiders Within: Writing on Transracial Adoption*. Respect to my Minnesota girlfriends who make it possible for me to stay in Korea, especially Jae Ran Kim, Shannon Gibney, Heewon Lee, Beth Kyong Lo, and Kim Park Nelson. Along with many of the aforementioned people, Kwok Sa-jin, Tobias Hübinette, Gregory Choy, and Jae-pyong Song gave sharp feedback on the manuscript. Finally, although there are far too many people working on various projects in the adoptee world to name individually, I would like to acknowledge the Seoul organizations: G.O.A'L, KoRoot, ASK, TRACK, and InKAS. And to my brother and sisters: for your courage in welcoming me home and in acknowledging me as a sister, and for the opportunity to try to mend our family, my sincerest thanks and enduring love.

Jane Jeong Trenka has won numerous awards for her writing. She is the author of *The Language of Blood*, called "original and beautifully written" by *Publishers Weekly*. She now lives in Korea.

Fugitive Visions is set in Arno Pro, a face designed by Robert Slimbach in the tradition of early Venetian book typefaces. Composition by BookMobile Design and Publishing Services, Minneapolis, Minnesota. Manufactured by Versa Press on acid-free paper.